Voice Massage

Scripts for Guided Imagery

Edited by
Denise Murray Edwards

Foreword by
James S. Gordon, MD

Oncology Nursing Society
Pittsburgh, PA

ONS Publishing Division
Publisher: Leonard Mafrica, MBA, CAE
Director, Commercial Publishing: Barbara Sigler, RN, MNEd
Production Manager: Lisa M. George
Technical Editor: Dorothy Mayernik, RN, MSN
Copy Editors: Toni Murray, Lori Wilson
Creative Services Assistant: Dany Sjoen

Voice Massage: Scripts for Guided Imagery

Copyright © 2002 by the Oncology Nursing Society

Library of Congress Control Number: 20022110961

ISBN 1-890504-30-0

Publisher's Note
This book is published by the Oncology Nursing Society (ONS). ONS neither represents nor guarantees that the practices described herein will, if followed, ensure safe and effective client care. The recommendations contained in this book reflect ONS's judgment regarding the state of general knowledge and practice in the field as of the date of publication. The recommendations may not be appropriate for use in all circumstances. Those who use this book should make their own determinations regarding specific safe and appropriate client-care practices, taking into account the personnel, equipment, and practices available at the hospital or other facility at which they are located. The editors and publisher cannot be held responsible for any liability incurred as a consequence from the use or application of any of the contents of this book. Figures and tables are used as examples only. They are not meant to be all-inclusive, nor do they represent endorsement of any particular institution by ONS. Mention of specific products and opinions related to those products do not indicate or imply endorsement by ONS.

ONS publications are originally published in English. Permission has been granted by the ONS Board of Directors for foreign translation. (Individual tables and figures that are reprinted or adapted require additional permission from the original source.) However, because translations from English may not always be accurate and precise, ONS disclaims any responsibility for inaccurate translations. Readers relying on precise information should check the original English version.

Printed in the United States of America

Oncology Nursing Society
Integrity • Innovation • Stewardship • Advocacy • Excellence • Inclusiveness

This book is dedicated to the many cancer survivors who have taught us much about the positive impact of imagery and have allowed us the privilege of sharing their journeys. We also wish to honor our clients who have used imagery to improve the quality of their lives in this world and have now found peace in the next. We give tribute to our colleagues, family, and friends who have shared their wisdom and helped us learn our truth. Finally, we dedicate this work to the researchers who have validated the scientific importance and efficacy of guided imagery in the healing process.

"We need strategies to reprogram the soft and changeable wirings of the brain in order to remember wellness."
—*Herbert Benson,* Timeless Healing *(1996)*

CONTRIBUTORS

Editor and Author

Denise Murray Edwards, RN, ARNP, MA, MEd, MTS
Mental Health Nurse Practitioner
The Center for Health and Well-Being
Iowa Health Systems
West Des Moines, IA
Introduction, Chapter 3. Scripts for Guided Imagery

Authors

Mary Jane Ott, MN, MA, RNCS
Advanced Practice Nurse
Pain and Palliative Care Program
Zakim Center for Integrated Therapies
Dana-Farber Cancer Institute
Boston, MA
Chapter 4. Guided Imagery Resources

Janice Post-White, RN, PhD, FAAN
Associate Professor
American Cancer Society
Professor of Oncology Nursing
University of Minnesota School of Nursing
Minneapolis, MN
Chapter 1. Clinical Indications for Use of Imagery in Oncology Practice

Mary L.S. Vachon, RN, PhD
Psychotherapist and Consultant in Private Practice
Clinical Consultant
Wellspring
Associate Professor
University of Toronto
Toronto, Ontario, Canada
Chapter 2. The Use of Imagery, Meditation, and Spirituality in the
Care of People With Cancer

CONTENTS

Imagery is the language of our emotions, our dreams, and our hopes. We learn it without effort and often turn to it without thought. The images that come to us may comfort us in difficult times, or, on the contrary, discourage us. We may "see" ourselves as doing well and feel content or focus on a troublesome aspect and feel uneasy.

This deep language can be used consciously to help us to explore the barriers in our own lives and the behaviors that keep us from doing or feeling as well as we might; to help us to endure uncomfortable procedures or pain; to mobilize our physiological functioning; and to show us ways to help or heal ourselves that may have eluded our conscious, thinking minds.

Nowhere have the uses of imagery been more fruitfully explored than in the field of cancer care. When, almost 30 years ago, I first heard about the imagery used by Carl Simonton, MD, a radiation oncologist, and his wife, Stephanie Matthews-Simonton, I was bowled over. The Simontons were helping clients with cancer to use images of white blood cells destroying cancer cells to enhance their clients' immune systems and, apparently, to mobilize their capacity for self-healing. They were, it appeared, teaching clients to use their minds to create representations that could improve their physical functioning and perhaps even alter the course of their disease.

The Simontons focused mostly on images of powerful immune cells attacking cancer cells. These were striking images and, for many people, effective ones. But they were visual and usually aggressive images. Imagery, I soon learned, could be auditory, kinesthetic, olfactory, and gustatory as well as visual. And images that were effective for cancer clients could be relaxing, explanatory, and renewing and nourishing as well as combative.

Over the years, we have made imagery a central part of our work at the Center for Mind-Body Medicine. We use imagery in the groups we have for people with cancer and other life-threatening illnesses, and we teach the uses of imagery in our Professional Training Program in MindBodySpirit Medicine. Imagery is a central element in the training we give to those who will become CancerGuides, health professionals who will help cancer clients make wise decisions about their cancer care and other factors that will shape their lives. Our annual Comprehensive Cancer Care Conference offers workshops about imagery, and they are always filled with clients as well as nurses, physicians, and mental health professionals. When I use images in our training, a sense of quietness and calm–of openness to my own sources of intuition, creativity, and self-healing–comes over me and seems to fill the room.

Nurses have been leaders in the use of imagery. It is an approach that is closely connected with the senses, the physical being of their clients, and the intimacy of nursing care. It also is closely connected to the nurse's function as teacher. Accustomed to helping their clients learn to care for themselves, nurses seem to find the work of helping their clients to form healing images particularly congenial.

This book of imagery scripts, edited by an oncology nurse, reflects many years of work by the authors, who also are nurses. It presents a range of imagery experiences that have been and can be used by those who care for people with cancer, images that can be easily learned and taught. Reading through the scripts, I am struck by the fact that imagery is not only the language of our bodily feelings and emotions, it also has the capacity to take us beyond ourselves–to show us the realms of peace, connection, and deep acceptance that we are accustomed to describing as spiritual.

As we read through the scripts, we learn to utilize our senses to mobilize the body's capacity for self-healing. We also learn to move so deeply into the senses that we are taken beyond them. At times, in learning to help others and helping ourselves with imagery, we may find the immediacy of the therapeutic moment opening into a healing that will alter our experience not only of illness, but of our lives.

Each time I lead exercises in guided imagery that are similar to those in this book–and I have done so on hundreds, perhaps thousands, of occasions–I feel myself feeling and learning more. And often I discover some part of myself that I did not know, until then, was thirsty for healing.

I'm grateful for this book and the lessons it teaches.

–James S. Gordon, MD, is director of the Center for Mind-Body Medicine in Washington, DC. He also is the author of *Comprehensive Cancer Care: Integrating Alternative, Complementary, and Conventional Therapies.*

ACKNOWLEDGMENTS

I want to begin by acknowledging the contributing authors who have shared the wisdom from their many years of working in the area of complementary medicine. Each brings a different perspective that enriches the whole. I am grateful to the clinicians who shared their scripts and offered them to all of us to use with clients. A special thank-you to Rene Ginder for her help with my fledgling computer skills and to Kathryn J. Curdue, MD, for her patient editorial assistance. The Psychoneuroimmunology Special Interest Group of the Oncology Nursing Society (ONS) provided inspiration and support, as did Barbara Sigler and Lisa George of the ONS Publishing Division. Finally, I want to acknowledge my husband, Warren P. Edwards, PhD, who shared the knowledge he has gleaned from many years of using scripts in his clinical practice and who read endless drafts of this book. His suggestions improved the clarity of this work.

Special thanks to the following individuals for contributing the guided imagery scripts that appear in Chapter 3.

Katherine Brown-Saltzman, RN, MA
Warren P. Edwards, PhD
Susan Ezra, RN, HNC
Gloria Green, RN, OCN®
Janith S. Griffith, RN, BSN, OCN®
Hazel A. Jackson, RN, MN
Redwing Keyssar, RN, BA, OCN®
Mary Joan Meyer, FSM
Patrice Rancour, MS, RN, CS
Joann Sanders, RNC, MS, CHTP
Judith A. Spross, PhD, RN
Monika Williamson, RN, BSN

—Denise Murray Edwards, RN, ARNP, MA, MEd, MTS

Visualizing Wellness

Several years ago, after leading a client in a session of progressive muscle relaxation (PMR), I hesitated before beginning a guided imagery. The script I had in mind involved an image of walking. Natalie, the client I was seeing for the first time, had undergone an above-the-knee amputation before beginning chemotherapy. However, all my intuition was telling me to continue, and I did. When Natalie opened her eyes following the experience, her first words were, "That was wonderful. It felt so good to walk freely, and I had hair." After a guided imagery session, I've come to expect the words "and I had hair" from the smiling lips of female clients and to see the joy, sometimes through tears, of remembered wellness.

Imagery is a form of behavior rehearsal, with a goal of relaxation, that includes a heightened sense of well-being. Although most clients are eventually able to experience the benefits of imagery by themselves, having a guide is helpful when learning the technique. Anyone can learn to be a guide, including friends and family members. It is a gift for a loved one to be able to play the role of healer; he or she moves from spectator to active member of the healing team. Once learned, imagery can be done anytime and anywhere, without worrying about a tape recorder or other equipment. Its reward is escape from whatever stresses the current environment holds. Imagery teaches the lesson of looking at the world with "soft eyes."

When I was a newly hired clinical specialist, 16 years ago, Mark was the first client referred to me. He had come to the Dana-Farber Cancer Institute for a second opinion, following a diagnosis of mesothelioma in the bases of both lungs and the lining of his abdominal cavity. Except for mild shortness of breath, Mark was experiencing no symptoms, and his oncologist had recommended no treatment until his disease progressed. In his early 60s, he wanted to live out his threescore years and 10. For him, 70 might be an acceptable age to die, but 60 was too young. After one physician suggested he go home and put his affairs in order, Mark began reading about alternative and complementary medicine and wanted to learn about relaxation and imagery.

During our initial meeting, Mark warned me that the army had rejected him, 40 years previously, for being too anxious. Here was a man who thrived on structured routine. He requested an hourly appointment at the same time each week. Time held an additional significance for him, because he had been told his life expectancy was six months. We talked about modifying his diet, increasing exercise, and identifying his triggers for stress. These themes were addressed many times in the ensuing months and years of our relationship.

Relaxation training began with PMR followed by guided imagery. Mark's breathing became slow and regular, his facial muscles softened, and he appeared relaxed. However, no images appeared in his mind's eye. As his ability to relax progressed and his breathing improved, he began again to play a wind instrument that he had set aside a few months prior to his diagnosis. Still, Mark was discouraged because he could never see anything in his mind. He was staring at a blank screen with no idea how to turn on the picture. In addition to his PMR practice, I began giving him homework assignments that included trips to the ocean, to museums, to fabric stores, and to the movie *Fantasia*.

One exquisitely beautiful spring morning, when Boston was alive with the smell of lilacs and glowing with spring flowers, I asked Mark what he noticed when driving to my office. His response was short and to the point: "I saw street signs." Then I asked him to close his eyes and describe my office and me. Time has blurred his exact response, but to him, a woman and a desk were the only prominent features.

Muscle relaxation and structured breathing exercises continued to go well as he faithfully practiced PMR twice a day and collected visual images. We continued to talk about fruits and vegetables and wheat grass along with hopes and dreams. Sometime in our third year of weekly meetings (except for those times I took vacation), I led Mark in guided imagery following some structured breathing. Suddenly, his face was transcendent. It was as if a door had opened in his mind to a new world full of colors and shapes, and that world was beautiful. As his new skill expanded and deepened through the years to follow, it was accompanied by a profound sense of well-being as he learned to see the world through soft eyes.

This is a story of healing, not cure. His cancer remained the same, neither shrinking nor growing. Because he continued to be without symptoms, chemotherapy was never initiated. In his 70th year, Mark died peacefully in his sleep. From him I learned a lot about imagery and perseverance and a little bit about caution when making a commitment to weekly meetings with a client with a "terminal" diagnosis.

In contrast to Mark, most people seem to need from two to four sessions to work with images they can later initiate independently. It is not a competition, and each person learns at a different pace.

There are a number of ways to introduce a client to guided imagery. Simply assessing the client for previous experiences using imagery for relaxation is a recommended first step. Successful experience forms an excellent foundation and provides direction for future uses of imagery. A second approach is to ask the client to describe a peaceful scene, assist the client in relaxation by using muscle relaxation or structured breathing, and direct or guide the individual in imagining the described scene.

This book will prepare you for a third approach. Using this strategy, the guide directs the image by using a prepared script. One significant benefit is a reduction in the client's performance anxiety, because the responsibility for the quality of the image is shifted from the client to the guide. This may engender a deeper relaxation than do other methods, because the client has permission to be passive whereas the guide both directs every step of the image and maintains the security of the environment. After the initial experience with a new script, the guide can modify specific details to fit the individual. In my experience, most people will adapt the words to fit their relaxation needs while they are listening.

Clients intuitively sort the components of an image and adopt what is most healing. A few years ago, I was directing an image with a client, Mike, who was a Vietnam combat veteran. The scene I was describing included a raft and water. Initially, Mike appeared to relax. Then I observed signs of rapid eye movement and facial tightness. Later he explained that, when I had said the word "raft," he had seen a raft in the Mekong Delta. He knew that wasn't the raft I wanted him to see, however, so he moved further back in time to a long-forgotten day spent with his brother as they fished and picnicked on a wooden raft on a quiet river in Maine. Mike spoke at length about the gift of this memory, and he soon bore little resemblance to the anxious man I had come to see in his hospital room. When I left, he was lifting the telephone to call his brother and talk about that childhood memory, what it meant to him then, and what it means to him now. Mike had used his mind to create an oasis of tranquillity in his high-tech, high-stress environment. Remembered wellness carries the seeds for calming strength.

In subsequent chapters of this book, you will learn about the art and science of imagery. Content will include indications for the use of imagery in oncology with emphasis on specific techniques for adults and children. A therapist who is a pioneer in the field of psychosocial oncology shares the images she used in her personal journey from diagnosis to remission and as she maintains wellness. In addition, generous clinicians have allowed reprinting of their scripts. Some of these scripts were developed to reduce specific symptoms, including pain, nausea, and anxiety. Others were developed to elicit the relaxation response. These scripts are yours to use for your own self-care and to promote healing in your clients.

Also included inside the back cover of the book is a compact disc titled *Guided Meditation,* which features meditations that I have recorded and music by Warren Edwards and Aaron Ginder. The recording was produced by the Center for Health and Well-Being at the Iowa Health System and has been reproduced with permission.

Chapter 1

Clinical Indications for Use of Imagery in Oncology Practice

Clinical Indications for Use of Imagery in Oncology Practice

Janice Post-White, RN, PhD, FAAN

Imagery is a mind-body intervention that uses the power of the imagination to access physical, emotional, and spiritual dimensions to effect change. Images employ six senses: visual, aural, tactile, olfactory, proprioceptive, and kinesthetic. Although imagery often is referred to as visualization, imagery includes imagining through any sense and not just being able to see something in the mind's eye. This concept is further developed in Chapter 3, "Scripts for Guided Imagery." Imagery can be practiced as an independent activity (self-hypnosis) or guided by a professional (guided imagery).

The importance of imagery is in its meaning to the individual experiencing it. Giving people with cancer permission to explore images and to acknowledge the feelings generated from the images fosters understanding and insight about how cancer has affected their lives. Insight provides a sense of empowerment and confidence as patients learn that they have some control over their responses and that there is something they can do to facilitate their own healing.

The most effective way to learn imagery is to practice it yourself, then bring it into your professional practice. Although professionals often use imagery therapeutically to help patients initiate a change in physical or emotional responses, images that spontaneously arise with no identified purpose can be equally as powerful as those that are created during therapy. Patients, particularly adults, often need to be reminded of the power of their own imaginations and their ability to create their responses to situations. This book offers the practitioner prepared scripts to use as guides for learning imagery and to build confidence in using imagery in practice. This chapter provides a rationale that explains why imagery may be effective and how imagery can be used to improve patient outcomes in clinical oncology practice.

BACKGROUND

Imagery has been described as "the world's oldest and greatest healing resource" (Achterberg, 1985, p. 3). Many ancient healing traditions use imagery to effect cure, alleviate suffering, and facilitate spiritual transformation. Traditionally, healers believed that imagery worked by allowing access to the patient's subconscious mind and by opening communication among the body, mind, and spirit. In the 1950s, the American Medical Association and the American Psychological Association recognized hypnosis, a type of imagery, as a therapeutic tool (Lee, 1999). Today, in modern health care, imagery is most commonly used in the form of guided imagery, clinical hypnosis, or self-hypnosis. Practitioners in various disciplines (e.g., nurses, physicians, and psychologists) use imagery and hypnosis in their practice for symptom management and enhancement of wellness. Stress-management programs use imagery to promote deep relaxation, to assist the client in gaining psychological insight, and to facilitate the achievement of mutual goals.

SCIENTIFIC BASIS

Imagery can be oriented to outcome, or end state, in which case the patient envisions a goal, such as being healthy and well. It also can be process-oriented, in which the patient imagines the mechanism of the desired effect (e.g., the action of a strong immune system fighting a viral infection or tumor). No evidence indicates that one form of imagery is more effective than another.

Although its exact mechanism of action is unknown, researchers believe that imagery modifies disease and reduces symptoms by reducing the stress response. In response to perceived stress, a cascade of signaling events causes the release of corticotropin-releasing hormone from the hypothalamus, adrenocorticotropic hormone from the pituitary gland, norepinephrine and epinephrine from the adrenal medulla and peripheral sympathetic nerve terminals, and immunosuppressive cortisol from the adrenal cortex. Serotonin and dopamine are two neurotransmitters that increase with stress and activate hypothalamic activity through receptor signaling (Black, 1995). Immune responses to emotional states are extremely complex. In general, acute stress temporarily increases plasma catecholamines and natural killer (NK) cell activity, whereas chronic stress suppresses NK cells and interleukin-1 beta (Cacioppo et al., 1998). Over time, chronic stress results in adrenal and immune suppression. Chronic stress may be the form of stress that is most harmful to cellular immune function, impairing the ability to ward off viruses and tumor cells (Pert, Dreher, & Ruff, 1998).

Although some evidence indicates that emotional reactivity to stress is regulated, in part, by genetic factors (Bonneau, Mormede, Vogler, McClearn, & Jones, 1998), other evidence indicates that individuals can modulate their response to stress. Extensive rat-model research by Robert Ader and Nicholas Cohen in the 1970s confirmed that expectations and beliefs can condition the immune system (Ader & Cohen, 1981; Ader, Felten, & Cohen, 1991). One of the goals of imagery is to reframe stressful situations so that, instead of eliciting the negative responses of fear and anxiety, they elicit positive images of healing and well-being (Dossey, 1995). Imagery also can be used to facilitate problem solving, increase a sense of control over the situation, foster emotional awareness, and restructure the meaning of a situation to reduce its perceived stressfulness.

IMAGERY TECHNIQUES

Imagery may be practiced independently, with a coach or teacher, or by watching a videotape or listening to an audiotape. The most effective imagery intervention is one that is specific to the patient's developmental age and desired outcomes and to his or her personality and preferences regarding relaxation and specific settings.

Imagery sessions for adults and adolescents are usually 10 to 30 minutes long. Most children can tolerate a 10- to 15-minute session.

A session typically begins with focused relaxation, or a meditative "centering" exercise, to help the patient become immersed in the present.

To facilitate centering, encourage slow and expansive breathing in which the breath moves lower into the chest and the abdominal muscles are more active in the breathing process than are the chest muscles. Relaxation helps to make the mind more susceptible to new information (Benson, 1993), but it is not required for imagery. Preschool and school-age children most often imagine in an active state; therefore, for them and other active imaginers, muscle relaxation is not necessarily a goal.

Once the patient is in a relaxed meditative state, the practitioner describes a relaxing, peaceful, or comforting image or introduces an image the patient suggested at an earlier time. Scenes commonly used to induce relaxation include clouds floating by, a sunset, sitting on a warm beach or by a fire on a snowy evening, or floating through water or space. Often, the scene is one that the client has actually experienced and found to be relaxing.

Children may prefer active images that involve motion, such as flying or playing a sport. Often, children do not like to close their eyes.

For active imagery, the practitioner guides the imagery, using positive suggestions to alleviate specific symptoms or conditions (i.e., evoking outcome, or end-state, imagery) or to rehearse or "walk through" a desired event (i.e., evoking process imagery). Images do not need to be correct in every detail or exact representations of a real physical state. Symbolic images may be the most powerful healing images because they are drawn from individual beliefs, culture, and meaning. For example, a 54-year-old woman with metastatic breast cancer watched her Alaskan husky dogs devour their breakfast and then used imagery to envision them scouring her body for tumor cells.

Throughout the imagery, the practitioner can encourage the patient to change the image in any way. Some people talk through the imagery and describe what they are experiencing. After a few minutes, the practitioner instructs the individual to return to the safe and peaceful place and to concentrate on being relaxed again. Following a few deep breaths, the person returns to full consciousness, ready to open his or her eyes and discuss the imagery. Thinking and talking about the imagery after the session is not necessary, but it may help the patient to interpret and make sense of the experience. Processing the imagery in this way facilitates acknowledgment of feelings and emotions associated with the imagery or situation. Such processing often provides guidance and suggestions for future sessions.

Although anyone can use imagery, people with higher self-hypnotic ability are better able to enter a meditative state and become involved or absorbed in the imagery. High hypnotizers (i.e., those who are easily hypnotized) recall pictures accurately, generate complex images, frequently recall dreams while in the waking state, and make few eye movements (Kwekkeboom, Huseby-Moore, & Ward, 1998).

Imagery has been used extensively with children and adolescents as well as with adults. Young children often are better at imagery than are adults because of their natural, active use of imagination. Researchers have found that hypnotizability rises through early childhood as language skills develop, peaks sometime from age 7 to age 14, and then levels off into adolescence and adulthood (Olness & Kohen, 1996). The practitioner must modify technique, session length, and type of imagery to match a child's developmental and cognitive age and personal preference.

PRECAUTIONS

The physical and emotional risks of mind-body techniques are practically nonexistent as long as the techniques are not used in place of conventional medicine (Goleman & Gurin, 1993). The literature presents few reports of imagery that produced adverse events. Kwekkeboom et al. (1998) reported increased anxiety in 3 of 15 subjects using imagery designed specifically to reduce anxiety associated with a stressful task. Van Fleet (2000) summarized negative effects from other studies and found that some patients felt a sense of loss of control with imagery, increased tension with music used in combination with imagery, and increased anxiety with efforts to relax. Because of the relaxation effect, some individuals with cardiovascular weakness experienced undesirable increased vasodilation and lowered blood pressure. Anecdotal accounts include reports of airway constriction or difficulty breathing when patients focused on breathing techniques. Changing the centering method (e.g., focusing on an object in the room rather than repeating a mantra) can help the patient to avoid this distressing re-sponse while still inducing relaxation. If a patient has an organic condition that compromises breathing, an effective relaxation-pro-moting intervention consists of instructing the patient to place his or her hands on the patient's chest or abdomen and to concentrate on the hands moving up and down as the patient breathes. Placing a hot-water bottle under the patient's hands can enhance the effective-ness of this intervention. These simple actions can de-emphasize breathing difficulty.

Evaluating patients prior to imagery and assessing them after-ward is strongly encouraged. Van Fleet (2000) cautioned that nurses should avoid using imagery with patients who have a history of psychiatric disorders, depression, or suicidal thoughts. Work with these patients and advanced techniques (e.g., age regression, depres-sion management) require further training for the clinician.

The expertise and training of the nurse should guide judgment in using imagery to achieve outcomes in practice. Imagery techniques can be quite easily applied to managing symptoms (e.g., pain, nau-sea, vomiting) and facilitating relaxation, sleep, or anxiety reduc-tion.

CLINICAL INDICATIONS AND OUTCOMES

Images evoke physical and emotional responses. Exploring these responses can help individuals to understand the meaning of the situ-ation or event the image represents. Achieving insight and making sense of the situation can contribute to problem solving or changing attitudes or behaviors. Using imagery to change negative expectations to positive ones is one example of how active imagery helps to reframe situations to reduce perceived stress and to empower the patient for participation in care. Imagery is not always intentional. Often, images appear spontaneously. Nothing specific needs to happen in imagery or as a result of imagery. The process itself stirs emotional responses that influence mind-body responses.

Imagery has been used therapeutically in a variety of conditions and populations. For example, imagery has been helpful to both adults and children who are dealing with pain and cancer.

Pain

Whether pain is from cancer, other illness, treatment side effects, injury, or physical stress, emotional factors contribute to pain perception. Mind-body interventions such as imagery can help to make the pain more manageable.

Stress, anxiety, and fatigue decrease the threshold of pain, making perceived pain more intense. Imagery can break this cycle of pain-tension-worry-anxiety-pain. Relaxation with imagery decreases pain directly by reducing muscle tension and related spasms. Imagery decreases pain indirectly by lowering anxiety and improving sleep, which influence pain perception. Imagery also is a distraction strategy. Vivid, detailed images using all senses tend to work best for pain control. In addition, cognitive reappraisal or restructuring used with imagery can increase a sense of control and power over the ability to reframe the meaning of pain.

Imagery is especially helpful in cases of pain related to muscle tension (e.g., some headaches and migraines) (Ilacqua, 1994). Imagery also can ease pain associated with childbirth (Rees, 1995), dental procedures, and surgery (Mandle, Jacobs, Arcari, & Domar, 1996; Manyande et al., 1995). Although highly hypnotizable people benefit more readily than others, practically all patients can learn to manage their pain and pain-related stresses better through simple imagery exercises (Spira & Spiegel, 1992).

Guided imagery has been used extensively with children to alleviate pain and anxiety (Lambert, 1999; Rusy & Weisman, 2000; Steggles, Damore-Petingola, Maxwell, & Lightfoot, 1997). Imagery is particularly helpful in getting a child through a medical procedure with a safe and effective level of sedation or analgesia and as little movement as possible. Suggestions to breathe deeply and to relax or be comfortable are combined with vivid images of a favorite place. It is best to introduce the child to breathing techniques and explore ideas about favorite places prior to the procedure. In critical or emergency situations, however, imagery has been successfully employed without prior work (Kohen, 2000).

Distraction imagery is most useful for handling severe pain that is exhausting and for dealing with painful procedures. Activities that draw attention away from physical pain include imagining the experience of floating or another pleasant sensation, recalling a pleasant past experience or feeling, or transferring attention from the pain source by rubbing fingers together or squeezing and releasing hands. Children can begin relaxation breathing by using a wand to blow bubbles.

Several studies document the effectiveness of imagery to reduce acute procedural pain in children. Broome, Rehwaldt, and Fogg (1998) taught relaxation, distraction, and imagery to 28 children and adolescents undergoing lumbar puncture (LP) for cancer treatment. Although staff observed little change in pain behaviors during LP, the children reported significant decreases in pain. Similarly, 30 children undergoing bone marrow biopsy who received either clinical hypnosis (relaxation and imagery followed by hypnotic suggestions to induce the feeling of anesthesia) or cognitive restructuring techniques with relaxation reported less pain and anxiety than did participants in a standard control group (Liossi & Hatira, 1999). For 26 children undergoing elective surgical procedures, preoperative imagery reduced postoperative pain scores and length of stay more effectively than did standard preoperative education; however, the amount of pain medication used was the same (Lambert, 1996). Two other studies measuring the effectiveness of imagery in reducing procedural pain in children with nonmalignant conditions found no differences in distress behaviors and pain with cardiac catheterization (Pederson, 1995) and during burn-dressing changes (Foertsch, O'Hara, Stoddard, & Kealey, 1998).

In cases of moderate pain, the focus of guided imagery is the alteration of the interpretation or perception of pain. Metaphors for pain can be used to dissociate from the pain and gain control (initially over the metaphor used), thereby reducing the intensity of the pain. For example, if the pain is described as intense, fiery, and red, the imagery can offer suggestions to change the color gradually to red-orange, orange, and then yellow. Suggestions to diffuse the color into space may reduce the intensity. Another alternative is to identify pleasant sensations with the metaphor. Associations with hot or cold temperature also can be used, with the individual concentrating on raising and lowering the intensity and associating pleasant sensations with different temperatures.

Focusing and transferring an image of analgesia is most effective for mild pain. Several techniques can be used, such as imagining the area being injected with anesthetic, being wooden, or being painted a color that numbs the area. Employing "hand-in-glove" anesthesia involves suggesting that the client imagine his or her hand entering a glove. As the fingers enter, they become numb. The palm also becomes numb when it is inside the glove. Transferring the sense of anesthesia to a painful area may be possible by suggesting that the client imagine touching the painful area with the gloved hand (Levitan, 1992). Although elements of relaxation, vividness, and distraction are important to pain reduction, Zachariae and Bjerring (1994) found that focused analgesia was the most effective in reducing acute pain, particularly when patients were highly hypnotizable.

Cancer Pain

Imagery interventions in oncology have focused on four areas: efficacy in pain management, influence on surgical outcomes, improvement in quality of life, and changes in immunity (Lee, 1999). Pain specific to cancer and its treatment can be acute or chronic.

In a randomized pretest-posttest study of 67 hospitalized patients with cancer pain, imagery combined with progressive muscle relaxation reduced pain sensation, intensity, and severity and decreased the use of nonopioid breakthrough analgesia (Sloman, 1995). Similarly, in two clinical trials involving bone marrow transplant recipients, investigators discovered that levels of mucositis-related pain were lower in the imagery group than in the group that did not employ imagery (Syrjala, Cummings, & Donaldson, 1992; Syrjala, Donaldson, Davis, Kippes, & Carr, 1995). In the trials, twice-weekly imagery sessions included progressive muscle relaxation (PMR), deep relaxation, transference of sensations, and individualized imagery.

Despite the frequency with which imagery is used in cancer treatment, few randomized controlled studies document its effectiveness in regard to reducing cancer-related pain (Wallace, 1997). However, a National Institutes of Health technology assessment panel recommended that behavioral therapies for chronic cancer pain be accepted as standard treatment and that reimbursement for these therapies be similar to reimbursement for medical treatments (Eastman, 1995). Kwekkeboom (1999) proposed a model to help to predict the effectiveness of cognitive-behavioral cancer-pain management strategies. In the model, factors influencing effectiveness included prior use of the strategies, perceived credibility of the strategies, and the degree of fit with the patient's preferred coping style. Research on specific interventions, outcomes affected by imagery, and factors influencing effectiveness is needed.

Symptom Management

Behavioral approaches for managing cancer-related symptoms have been the focus of systematic research since the early 1980s (Simonton & Sherman, 1998). The symptoms most relevant to cancer care include nausea and vomiting, anxiety, hot flashes, fatigue, depression, and insomnia. Problems with wound healing also are common in regard to cancer care.

For years patients have used imagery to combat chemotherapy-induced nausea and vomiting (Burish & Jenkins, 1992; Frank, 1985; Troesch, Rodehaver, Delaney, & Yanes, 1993). Research on relaxation and imagery to promote relief from nausea and vomiting has included the study of PMR and calming imagery, which most often are administered over one to three brief sessions. Controlled studies suggested that imagery is effective in reducing nausea and vomiting, along with anxiety and autonomic arousal, during and immediately following chemotherapy (Simonton & Sherman, 1998).

Research on the effectiveness of imagery in reducing symptoms other than nausea and vomiting is limited. Fatigue is one of the most common side effects of cancer and cancer treatment, but studies to determine the effectiveness of fatigue-reducing interventions are still under way. Anecdotal reports, however, support the use of imagery in reducing fatigue and improving energy levels following treatment.

Imagery has been used to reduce hot flashes secondary to hormonal therapies. One study demonstrated significant reductions in frequency and intensity with just one session of home practice of relaxation training (Domar, Irvin, & Mills, 1997). Imagery also has been used during radiation therapy to reduce symptoms and increase a sense of comfort (Kolcaba & Fox, 1999).

Emotional and Spiritual Effects

The word *cancer* evokes powerful images, usually negative ones (Brown-Saltzman, 1997). Imagery can be effective in changing a patient's focus, transferring it from side effects (e.g., nausea, hair loss, fatigue, fear of death) to inner beauty, strength, and the ability to overcome adversity. Suggestions for building on the positive aspects of relationships, support, and connectedness with others can help patients to reframe their emotional responses, transforming them into positive ones. Imagery also can be used to explore meaning in cancer and its role in the individual's life. Although processing these images may be difficult for the patient and practitioner, it is an important part of moving forward in response to illness.

If the patient and practitioner are comfortable with prayer, prayer combined with imagery can induce a calming and peaceful state. Such an approach is particularly beneficial at the end of life or when pain or symptoms are overwhelming. Being an active participant in imagery takes energy. Relatively passive imagery, such as that used with prayer, may be more effective than active imagery. Simple blessings, prayers for strength or relief from pain, touch, or meditative prayer can be powerful and meaningful for patients, family members, and practitioners. Katherine Brown-Saltzman (1997) described the sense of peace and reassurance, accompanied by deep relaxation, that resulted from using silent meditative prayer along with the image of salmon swimming upstream, a metaphor for the patient's own stem cells returning home after transplantation. A script titled "Hope Kindled" by Brown-Saltzman, which appears in Chapter 3, demonstrates such imagery. According to Brown-Saltzman, "prayer and imagery are two ways to fill the spirit" (p. 259).

Cancer Outcomes

Several prospective randomized studies found that imagery increased the survival rate of patients with cancer (Fawzy et al., 1993; Grossarth-Maticek & Eysenck, 1989; Spiegel, Bloom, Kraemer, & Gottheil, 1989; Walker, 1998). Many other factors can influence cancer outcomes. Psychosocial factors (e.g., depression) (Walker) and diagnostic factors (e.g., stage of disease) (Ratcliffe, Dawson, & Walker, 1995) are consistent covariates in regard to explaining survival outcomes.

A common explanation of how imagery may improve cancer outcomes postulates that imagery increases cellular immune function. Some studies have demonstrated increases in NK cytotoxicity (Fawzy et al., 1990, 1993; Gruber et al., 1993; Gruber, Hall, Hersh, & Dubois,

1988; Walker et al., 1996) and T cell responses (Gruber et al., 1988, 1993); others have found no differences (Post-White et al., 1996; Richardson et al., 1997) or decreases (Zachariae et al., 1994) in the number of NK cells and their cytotoxicity. Despite inconclusive effects on cancer outcome, imagery interventions have consistently improved patients' coping responses and psychological states (Post-White et al.; Richardson et al.). This suggests that imagery mediates psychoneuroimmune outcomes relating to cancer.

Further study is needed to determine the clinical significance of immunologic effects as well as the long-term effects and mechanisms of action. Do psychoneuroimmune responses to imagery influence clinical outcomes and quality of life? How do these responses mediate psychosocial and clinical outcomes? Measuring clinical outcomes relevant to quality of life and health and illness is critical to demonstrating cost-effectiveness and the efficacy of imagery in practice.

SUMMARY

Imagery can have a measurable effect on symptoms related to cancer. Imagery has been extensively used to reduce acute procedural pain and chronic pain and has reduced nausea and vomiting, anxiety, and depression. Improvements in coping and in overall sense of quality of life also have been measured in patients with cancer using imagery. More study is needed, however, to demonstrate effects on immune function and whether these changes have clinical significance.

Having cancer and undergoing cancer treatment result in physical, emotional, and spiritual distress. Imagery is an independent nursing intervention that can reduce the perceived stressfulness of undergoing cancer treatment, empower patients with a specific skill to combat symptoms and distress, and provide a sense of hope for strength and motivation throughout the cancer journey.

REFERENCES

Achterberg, J. (1985). *Imagery in healing: Shamanism and modern medicine.* Boston: Shambhala.

Ader, R., & Cohen, N. (1981). Conditioned immunopharmacologic responses. In R. Ader (Ed.), *Psychoneuroimmunology* (pp. 281–319). New York: Academic Press.

Ader, R., Felten, D.L., & Cohen, N. (1991). *Psychoneuroimmunology* (2nd ed.). San Diego: Academic Press.

Benson, H. (1993). The relaxation response. In D. Goleman & J. Gurin (Eds.), *Mind/body medicine* (pp. 233–258). Yonkers, NY: Consumer Reports Books.

Black, P.H. (1995). Psychoneuroimmunology: Brain and immunity. *Scientific American Science and Medicine, 2*(6), 16–25.

Bonneau, R.H., Mormede, P., Vogler, G.P., McClearn, G.E., & Jones, B.C. (1998). A genetic basis for neuroendocrine-immune interactions. *Brain, Behavior, and Immunity, 12,* 83–89.

Broome, M.E., Rehwaldt, M., & Fogg, L. (1998). Relationships between cognitive behavioral techniques, temperament, observed distress, and pain reports in children and adolescents during lumbar puncture. *Journal of Pediatric Nursing, 13*(1), 48–51.

Brown-Saltzman, K. (1997). Replenishing the spirit by meditative prayer and guided imagery. *Seminars in Oncology Nursing, 13,* 255–259.

Burish, T.G., & Jenkins, R.A. (1992). Effectiveness of biofeedback and relaxation training in reducing the side effects of cancer chemotherapy. *Health Psychology, 11*(1), 17–23.

Cacioppo, J.T., Berntson, G.G., Malarkey, W.B., Kiecolt-Glaser, J.K., Sheridan, J.F., Poehlmann, K.M., et al. (1998). Autonomic, neuroendocrine, and immune responses to psychological stress: The reactivity hypothesis. *Annals of the New York Academy of Sciences, 1,* 664–673.

Domar, A.D., Irvin, J., & Mills, D. (1997). Use of relaxation training to reduce the frequency and intensity of tamoxifen-induced hot flashes. *Mind/Body Medicine, 2*(2), 82–86.

Dossey, B. (1995). Complementary modalities, part 3: Using imagery to help your patient heal. *American Journal of Nursing, 96*(6), 41–47.

Eastman, P. (1995). Panel endorses behavioral therapy for cancer pain. *Journal of the National Cancer Institute, 87,* 1666–1667.

Fawzy, F.I., Fawzy, N., Hyun, L.S., Elashoff, R., Guthrie, D., Fahy, J.L., et al. (1993). Malignant melanoma: Effects of an early structured psychiatric intervention, coping and affective state on recurrence and survival 6 years later. *Archives of General Psychiatry, 50,* 681–689.

Fawzy, F.I., Kemeny, M.E., Fawzy, N.W., Elashoff, M.D., Cousins, N., & Fahey, J.L. (1990). A structured psychiatric intervention for cancer patients II. Changes over time in immunological measures. *Archives of General Psychiatry, 47,* 729–735.

Foertsch, C.E., O'Hara, M.W., Stoddard, F.J., & Kealey, G.P. (1998). Treatment-resistant pain and distress during pediatric burn-dressing changes. *Journal of Burn Care and Rehabilitation, 19,* 219–224.

Frank, J. (1985). The effect of music therapy and guided imagery on chemotherapy induced nausea and vomiting. *Oncology Nursing Forum, 12,* 47–52.

Goleman, D., & Gurin, J. (Eds.). (1993). *Mind-body medicine.* Yonkers, NY: Consumer Reports Books.

Grossarth-Maticek, R., & Eysenck, H.J. (1989). Length of survival and lymphocyte percentage in women with mammary cancer as a function of psychotherapy. *Psychological Reports, 65,* 315–321.

Gruber, B.L., Hall, N.R., Hersh, S.P., & Dubois, P. (1988). Immune system and psychologic changes in metastatic cancer patients while using ritualized relaxation and guided imagery: A pilot study. *Scandinavian Journal of Behavioral Therapy, 17,* 25–46.

Gruber, B.L., Hersh, S.P., Hall, N.R., Waletzky, L.R., Kunz, J.F., Carpenter, J.K., et al. (1993). Immunological responses of breast cancer patients to behavioral interventions. *Biofeedback and Self Regulation, 18*(1), 1–22.

Ilacqua, G.E. (1994). Migraine headaches: Coping efficacy of guided imagery training. *Headache, 34*(2), 99–102.

Kohen, D. (2000, June). *Integrating hypnosis into practice.* Presentation of the University of Minnesota and the Minnesota Society of Clinical Hypnosis at the Introductory Workshop in Clinical Hypnosis, St. Paul, MN.

Kolcaba, K., & Fox, C. (1999). The effects of guided imagery on comfort of women with early stage breast cancer undergoing radiation therapy. *Oncology Nursing Forum, 26,* 67–72.

Kwekkeboom, K. (1999). A model for cognitive-behavioral interventions in cancer pain management. *Image: Journal of Nursing Scholarship, 31,* 151–156.

Kwekkeboom, K., Huseby-Moore, K., & Ward, S. (1998). Imaging ability and effective use of guided imagery. *Research in Nursing and Health, 21,* 189–198.

Lambert, S. (1996). The effects of hypnosis/guided imagery on the postoperative course of children. *Developmental and Behavioral Pediatrics, 17,* 307–310.

Lambert, S. (1999). Distraction, imagery, and hypnosis: Techniques for management of children's pain. *Journal of Child and Family Nursing, 2*(1), 5–15.

Lee, R. (1999). Guided imagery as supportive therapy in cancer treatment. *Alternative Medicine Alert, 2*(6), 61–64.

Levitan, A.A. (1992). The use of hypnosis with cancer patients. *Psychiatric Medicine, 10*(1), 119–131.

Liossi, C., & Hatira, P. (1999). Clinical hypnosis versus cognitive behavioral training for pain management with pediatric cancer patients undergoing bone marrow aspirations. *International Journal of Clinical Hypnosis, 47*(2), 104–116.

Mandle, C.L., Jacobs, S.G., Arcari, P.M., & Domar, A.D. (1996). The efficacy of relaxation response interventions with adult patients: A review of the literature. *Journal of Cardiovascular Nursing, 10*(3), 4–26.

Manyande, A., Berg, S., Gettins, D., Stanford, S.C., Mazhero, S., Marks, D.F., et al. (1995). Preoperative rehearsal of active coping imagery influences subjective and hormonal responses to abdominal surgery. *Psychosomatic Medicine, 57*(2), 177–182.

Olness, K., & Kohen, D. (1996). *Hypnosis and hypnotherapy with children* (3rd ed.). New York: Guilford Press.

Pederson, C. (1995). Effect of imagery on children's pain and anxiety during cardiac catheterization. *Journal of Pediatric Nursing, 10,* 365–374.

Pert, C.B., Dreher, H.E., & Ruff, M.R. (1998). The psychosomatic network: Foundations of mind-body medicine. *Alternative Therapies, 4*(4), 30–41.

Post-White, J., Schroeder, L., Hannahan, A., Johnston, M.K., Salscheider, N., & Grandt, N. (1996). Response to imagery/support in breast cancer survivors. *Oncology Nursing Forum, 23,* 355.

Ratcliffe, M.A., Dawson, A.A., & Walker, L.G. (1995). Personality inventory L-scores in patients with Hodgkin's disease and non-Hodgkin's lymphoma. *Psycho-oncology, 4,* 39–45.

Rees, B.L. (1995). Effect of relaxation with guided imagery on anxiety, depression, and self-esteem in primiparas. *Journal of Holistic Nursing, 13,* 255–267.

Richardson, M.A., Post-White, J., Grimm, E.A., Moye, L.A., Singletary, S.E., & Justice, B. (1997). Coping, life attitudes, and immune responses to imagery and group support after breast cancer. *Alternative Therapies in Health and Medicine, 3*(5), 62–70.

Rusy, L.M., & Weisman, S.J. (2000). Complementary therapies for acute pediatric pain management. *Pediatric Clinics of North America, 47,* 589–599.

Simonton, S.S., & Sherman, S.C. (1998). Psychological aspects of mind-body medicine: Promises and pitfalls from research with cancer patients. *Alternative Therapies in Health and Medicine, 4*(4), 50–67.

Sloman, R. (1995). Relaxation and the relief of cancer pain. *Nursing Clinics of North America, 30,* 697–709.

Spiegel, D., Bloom, J.R., Kraemer, H.C., & Gottheil, E. (1989). Effect of psychosocial treatment on survival of patients with metastatic breast cancer. *Lancet, 2,* 888–891.

Spira, J.L., & Spiegel, D. (1992). Hypnosis and related techniques in pain management. *Hospice Journal, 8*(1–2), 89–119.

Steggles, S., Damore-Petingola, S., Maxwell, J., & Lightfoot, N. (1997). Hypnosis for children and adolescents with cancer: An annotated bibliography 1985–1995. *Journal of Pediatric Oncology Nursing, 14*(1), 27–32.

Syrjala, K.L., Cummings, C., & Donaldson, G.W. (1992). Hypnosis or cognitive behavioral training for the reduction of pain and nausea during cancer treatment: A controlled clinical trial. *Pain, 48,* 137–146.

Syrjala, K.L., Donaldson, G.W., Davis, M.W., Kippes, M.E., & Carr, J.E. (1995). Relaxation and imagery and cognitive-behavioral training reduce pain during cancer treatment: A controlled clinical trial. *Pain, 63,* 189–198.

Troesch, L.M., Rodehaver, C.B., Delaney, E.A., & Yanes, B. (1993). The influence of guided imagery on chemotherapy-related nausea and vomiting. *Oncology Nursing Forum, 20,* 1179–1185.

Van Fleet, S. (2000). Relaxation and imagery for symptom management: Improving patient assessment and individualizing treatment. *Oncology Nursing Forum, 27,* 501–509.

Walker, L.G. (1998). Hypnosis and cancer: Host defenses, quality of life and survival. *Contemporary Hypnosis, 15*(1), 34–38.

Walker, L.G., Miller, I., Walker, M.B., Simpson, E., Ogston, K., Segar, A., et al. (1996). Immunological effects of relaxation training and guided imagery in women with locally advanced breast cancer. *Psycho-oncology, 5*(3 Suppl. 5), 16.

Wallace, K. (1997). Analysis of recent literature concerning relaxation and imagery interventions for cancer pain. *Cancer Nursing, 20*(2), 79–87.

Zachariae, R., & Bjerring, P. (1994). Laser-induced pain-related brain potentials and sensory pain ratings in high and low hypnotizable subjects during hypnotic suggestions of relaxation, dissociated imagery, focused analgesia, and placebo. *International Journal of Clinical and Experimental Hypnosis, XLII*(1), 56–80.

Zachariae, R., Hansen, J.B., Andersen, M., Jinquan, T., Petersen, K.S., Simonsen, C., et al. (1994). Changes in cellular immune function after immune specific guided imagery and relaxation in high and low hypnotizable healthy subjects. *Psychotherapy and Psychosomatics, 61*(1–2), 74–92.

Chapter 2

The Use of Imagery, Meditation, and Spirituality in the Care of People With Cancer

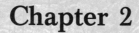

The Use of Imagery, Meditation, and Spirituality in the Care of People With Cancer

Mary L.S. Vachon, RN, PhD

Life unfolds in interesting ways. Denise Murray Edwards, RN, CS, ARNP, MA, MEd, MTS, the editor of this book, has been a friend of mine since grade 2, when we both attended St. Pius V School in Lynn, MA. We were debating partners at St. Mary's Girls' High School and never needed to discuss much with one another because we thought in such similar ways. I think that I had a role in Denise's decision to become a nurse, but we couldn't go to the same university because of financial considerations. Denise headed off to Boston College, and I went to Massachusetts General Hospital and Northeastern University, a move that had a significant positive impact on my nursing career.

Denise's path and mine seemed to have headed in different directions—that is, until 1985, when I received the Mara Mogensen Flaherty Memorial Lectureship Award of the ONS Foundation. Denise saw my picture in the Oncology Nursing Society's journal, *Oncology Nursing Forum,* and contacted me. We both had become psychiatric nurses working in oncology, both had worked in the area of psychosocial adjustment to cancer, both were therapists working with patients with cancer, and both had worked in the area of occupational stress. Our paths had actually been parallel; now they had an opportunity to converge.

I visited Denise at the Dana-Farber Cancer Institute, where she was working at the time, to participate in a guided imagery course. In my first guided visualization experience, I tried to go mentally to a particular beach in Hawaii. But, as I was making myself comfortable there, the scene suddenly switched, and I was at Makena Beach on Maui. I had visited Makena Beach in 1987 in my visualizations. Makena

Beach has become my very special personal paradise, a place to which I often have returned in personal visualizations. I visited my beach in reality in March 1997, the first anniversary of being declared in remission from my stage IV lymphoma. Denise had a role to play in that real trip, as well–but I'm getting ahead of myself.

The coincidences that have characterized my relationship with Denise are just examples of the synchronicity that has characterized my professional life as an oncology nurse and my own experience as a patient with cancer. I experienced a spontaneous spiritual transformation as a result of my cancer experience. In the search to understand what was happening, I became more involved in the use of imagery and other spiritual techniques. During the spiritual transformation, a number of unusual experiences occurred. I have been told this is part of a mystical experience (Kason, 2000). I believe that my use of imagery and other spiritually therapeutic techniques helped me to recognize significant patterns and, in some way, helped them to happen.

In this chapter, I will present two case studies that show how imagery and spiritual work affected the experience of cancer. The first study is my own story; the second, the story of one of my clients. I then will turn to the topics of cancer as a spiritually transforming experience, the impact of spirituality on my clinical work, and the implications of my experience for oncology nurses.

CASE STUDY 1: ME

In September 1996, I was at the Terminal Care Conference in Montreal. This is a meeting that I often attend, but that year my experience was different. I kept getting closed out of the "intellectual" meetings I would generally attend; true to form, I had neglected to register for workshops and breakout sessions. I sulked, thinking that I would just go back to my hotel room and work on an article. Instead, I went to several of the "stupid" spiritual meetings that were being held. Each time I did this, I found that I really got something out of the meeting.

In one meeting, I began to get "messages" in my head–messages saying that I needed to go back to church and that I needed to spend time doing meditation and yoga at Wellspring, a community-based support program for people with cancer. (I am one of the cofounders of Wellspring, and I do weekly crisis intervention there.) I was getting the message that I needed to have new topics for my presentations, that I needed new topics for research, and that life was going to be different.

During this time, my feet were really bothering me. I also became aware of some minor abdominal pain, 1 to 2 on a 10-point scale, but my feet—at a 4 or 5—were causing me more concern. I made an appointment to be fitted for orthotics. (Only later, after starting treatment with chemotherapy and allopurinol, did the foot problem go away. What I did not know while at the conference was that lymphoma cells had accumulated in my feet.) To deal with the abdominal pain, I called my family physician's office for an appointment. I didn't really push the secretary about my abdominal pain; I waited a couple weeks until it was convenient for me to visit the doctor. I was sure that I had an ulcer, just like my friend Bonnie, who had been diagnosed with an ulcer a few months previously.

My doctor was to see me on October 2, the first anniversary of my mother's death. October 2 also is the Feast of the Guardian Angels. I remember being amused when I learned of the angels' feast day. I hadn't thought about angels since my Catholic girlhood. One of my sisters gave family members angel pins to wear for the wake and funeral. I brought mine back to Toronto to wear as a mourning pin for the first 30 days after my mother's death. Before leaving for a business meeting, I lent the pin to one of my clients who was suicidal. The pin was to be a reminder that I would be thinking of her while I was away and that I, unlike the family members whose deaths she was mourning, would return. My client returned the pin when I came back and said that she felt that my mother had kept her from committing suicide. My sisters and I exchanged angels as gifts to one another, and I began to develop a small collection of them. I thought about angels a lot more after my diagnosis as I found myself surrounded by them.

I ended up not seeing my doctor until October 9; she ordered an ultrasound to diagnose the cause of my abdominal pain. I went to my ultrasound appointment sure that I had an ulcer. I came out with a tentative diagnosis of lymphoma or "metastatic something else." Lymphoma was the better option.

As I found myself hoping that I had lymphoma, the faces of many clients began to dance before my eyes. Some of the clients I was thinking of were alive, but many were dead.

I rapidly became more symptomatic. By the next week, when I could get an appointment for a computed tomography (CT) scan, it was clear that there was something in my chest as well. I was quickly diagnosed with stage III intermediate-grade lymphoma, a diagnosis that was changed to stage IV when the apparently benign lesions in my liver and lungs disappeared with chemotherapy.

I explained to the radiologist who read my CT scan that I was about to head off to Hong Kong and Shanghai to give lectures: "Breaking Bad News" and "Women With Cancer" among them. I told him I thought that he had done a very good job of breaking bad news and that I would mention him in my presentation.

I must confess that, in the early days of my diagnosis, I thought that people would probably assume that I would die. I considered death an impending reality. I began to think about my funeral. What would be the best way for my huge family to travel from Massachusetts to Toronto? Or should there be two funerals, one in Toronto and one in Massachusetts?

I thought that, given my guarded prognosis, it wouldn't be surprising if I were chosen to receive awards before I died. I wondered how I could use this cancer experience to help other people with cancer.

At one point in the early days, a client who does Silva Mind Control had my name sent into the universe. A message came back: There was something that I had yet to learn. Reflecting back on this, I began to realize that my cancer experience was intended to teach me, and I was already beginning to learn what I needed to know. I thought a diagnosis of cancer was a bit of a dramatic way to get me to go back to church, but I got the message and went back.

Needless to say, some of my treatment team, friends, and colleagues questioned my judgment in heading to China four days after having my first chemotherapy. But the trip was to be a family affair, with my husband, son, and daughter coming along. I was scheduled to lecture about anger, anticipatory grief, loss, and bereavement with my son, a ninth-grade dropout and former street kid who had just graduated from university with distinction. I figured that, if this was going to be my last lecture, what could be better than to pass the torch of lecturing to the next generation. I come from a family of Boston-Irish politicians; public speaking is in our genes.

Synchronicities and Other Unusual Experiences

It was in Hong Kong that the "unusual" things began to happen—unless, of course, you feel that it wasn't at all unusual that the Third Hong Kong International Congress and Seventh International EBV Symposium, at which I was to be speaking, happened to include many of the world's most prominent lymphoma specialists. There was no problem finding someone to agree to handle any medical problems that might arise. My persistent cough during the meeting may have been an irritant to the group as well as a not-too-subtle reminder that none of us knows what the future will hold.

Midway through the convention, I was standing in a line and happened to look down at a display rack of pamphlets. I saw a pamphlet about lymphoma. As I reached for this information I now needed, I noticed that the rack was in the booth for Neupogen® (Amgen, Inc., Thousand Oaks, CA). I was taking Neupogen to keep my white blood cell count up while traveling. By the next morning, the label on my Neupogen bottle had changed color, showing that it had been frozen in transit. Now the drug was useless. The booth presented a solution to my problem of getting a replacement supply. With the help of the Amgen representatives, I had a new supply within hours. At that time, Neupogen was not yet available in Hong Kong. I had the feeling that my finding the Amgen booth was more than a mere coincidence.

During chemotherapy I was conscious of all the support that I was receiving from friends, relatives, and colleagues. I listed all their good wishes in my social support book. I was conscious that there were "others" accompanying me as well. I became aware that I was being accompanied through the process by an aura of what I could best describe as "people from the other side." Generally, I didn't talk about this because I knew that it sounded strange. When I did speak about it, people asked if I knew who was there. My feeling was that I didn't know, and I was hesitant to name anyone because there might be people I wasn't even thinking about who were present to me at this time.

Midway through my chemotherapy, I went for a CT scan. I started to meditate, and a prayer from my childhood came: " . . . all the angels and saints and you, my brothers and sisters, to pray for me to the Lord, Our God." I became conscious that my brother, Richard, who died when I was 3, was part of my support team. I suspected that my parents, also both deceased, were part of the group, too.

I reflected about the fact that, over the years, clients have been my best teachers. What I learned from Ann, I passed on to Ruth, what I learned from Ruth, I passed onto Deb. I was aware that I was but a channel for the many experiences and "learnings" received from clients over almost 30 years of working with people with cancer and those who are bereaved. It was as though my clients were now walking with me. There also was a calmness about me during the chemotherapy, which was quite unusual. Usually, I am a somewhat assertive (some might even call me aggressive) person.

During chemotherapy, I went back to church and also did yoga and mind-body meditation, as the message had said I should do. I also began qi gong, a Chinese form of exercise whose purpose is to heal and increase vitality. Long-term cancer survivors in Shanghai had introduced me to this exercise. Later I found out that all these practices could open one up to spiritually transformative experiences (STEs) (Kason, 2000).

Each time I went to church, the priest would say something I needed to hear or something in the bulletin would speak directly to me. It was getting a bit weird, but it was helpful, as well. It was particularly helpful when Father Rosica spoke about the final scene in *Les Misérables,* when Valjean is dying. All the people from his past return to be with him. This was his best understanding of the Communion of Saints. This helped me to conceptualize what I was experiencing within a framework that I could understand. Why it should be happening to me, however, was still beyond me.

One day in April 1997, I was driving to work and became conscious that my angels, as I had come to think of them, were no longer quite as close to my head. They had moved a couple of energy fields away. I gave them permission to move, chuckling to myself that this whole thing was bizarre.

While on that drive, I was thinking that I was probably going to need to have a stem cell transplant. If this were the case, I needed to pay down my credit line. I needed $5,000.

I went to work and had a meeting in which I discussed my some-what ambiguous role in palliative care in the setting in which I was then working. I left the meeting aware that the role I thought I was meant to have was clearly not the role I was to have. As I walked back to my office, I reflected and tried to get some perspective on my life and professional role. I thought that I didn't know whether I would need a stem cell transplant soon. If I did, I didn't know if I would survive or die. I reflected that, in the time I had left, I should focus my efforts on the clients with whom I was working. I should forget the fact that, previously, I had had an international reputation for my work in palliative care and occupational stress. Those days were over. They had been wonderful, but they were part of the past. The future was a big question mark. I should remember that I had always been sustained professionally by my work with clients. Now, if my time was limited and I still considered that it was important to work, then I should focus my efforts on trying to help to make a difference in the lives of those whose paths were crossing mine.

I returned to my office and received a telephone call informing me of a new award in palliative care. The award was named after my good friend, Dorothy Ley, MD. Eleven people had been nominated, and I was to be the first recipient of the award. The first part of the award was a print by artist-author Robert Pope, which I cherish. I have taken Pope's work, in the form of his book *Illness and Healing: Images of Cancer* (Pope, 1991), around the world in my presentations. (Pope succumbed to the late effects of Hodgkin's disease.) I also received, as part of the Ley award, a nice plaque and a check for $5,000. Mentally, I thanked Dorothy Ley and recognized her as being one of the people on the other side who had come to accompany me on my journey. It wasn't surprising she was with me; we were kindred spirits in many ways.

In May, I was having a healing touch session. Ava, the therapist, told me to go to my peaceful place. I went to my beach in Maui. At the end of the session, she asked when I was last in Hawaii. I said that it was years ago, "but, trust me, I'm not travel-deprived." As I walked away, I realized that the subject of Hawaii had come up twice in the last two weeks. Maybe I should think about going to Hawaii next winter. Within six days, I received an invitation to lecture in Hawaii the next March. That invitation put me on the beach on Maui on the first anniversary of being in remission.

Several weeks after I received the invitation, I was speaking with Denise. She asked if I had received an invitation to speak in Hawaii–she had recommended me. She was responsible for sending me back to the beach that was so significant in my first visualization, which occurred when I was in a course with her. We have been in sync for a long time.

The day after going to my beach to celebrate being in remission, I found the perfect card to celebrate the occasion. It had a picture of my beach and gold writing that said, "Heaven can wait. I've found Maui." I bought several of those cards and sent them to my oncologist, primary nurses, chemo nurses, and support team.

In June 1997, our daughter decided that she wanted to go to college in New York instead of rolling out of bed and going to the school down the street as she originally intended. Supporting a daughter in U.S. dollars with Canadian "dollarettes" seemed an insurmountable obstacle. The next month, I found that I had stage IV disease and that I probably needed an immediate stem cell transplant. Then, suddenly, my pathology changed and polymerase-chain reaction testing showed that I had no BCL2 and that I might be cured.

The next week, I was appointed as a consumer representative to a national committee. The stipend made my daughter's tuition seem only ridiculous instead of totally crazy.

Things were really getting weird. I just needed to think something and it would come to me. Money that I needed would appear. Anything I needed just seemed to materialize. I got comfort from *Diary of a Death Professional* (Underwood, 1995) that a friend and colleague, Hannelore Wass, PhD, had sent me when I was first diagnosed. The author, Merlys Underwood, PhD, a death educator diagnosed with several cancers, wrote that, whenever she was about to be diagnosed with a new cancer, synchronicities would begin to happen. I later read in *Awakening Intuition* (Schultz, 1998) that, at times of change, holes can develop in one's energy layers through which spirits can enter to provide guidance and do their work.

In the middle of all this, I took a course on spirituality offered at Wellspring by Reverend Doug Graydon and Helen Brent, a volunteer and social worker who was a long-time meditator. This course got me to integrate prayer into my life in a way I hadn't previously.

ASIST and the Prayer Wheel

I knew that I needed to speak with someone about my experiences. I thought that the only person who would understand was Michael Kearney, MD, a hospice physician from Ireland who wrote *Mortally Wounded: Stories of Soul Pain, Death, and Healing* (Kearney, 1996). I sent him a psychic message, testing my powers and telling him to invite me to Ireland. Even as I did this, I knew that traveling to Ireland for a consultation was not the answer. I needed to speak with someone locally. The name of a former colleague, a psychiatrist, John Rossiter-Thornton, MD, came to my mind. I hadn't thought about him in years, since we both had left the Clarke Institute of Psychiatry. Within a few weeks, we were both at a complementary medicine meeting of the Ontario Medical Association. I told him that I had recently thought about him, that some strange things had been happening since I had been diagnosed with lymphoma, and that I needed to speak with someone about this. He said that he had recently developed a new form of therapy that he thought might be helpful. "The ASIST (A Self-directed Inner Search Therapy) technique allows participants—with the therapist's help—to access their nonconscious mind (i.e., anything not currently in the conscious mind) at will" (Rossiter-Thornton, 2000, p. 128).

ASIST is a form of meditation to be guided by trained psychotherapists only. To date, only a few psychotherapists have been trained in this method. Dr. Rossiter-Thornton plans to train other psychotherapists to use this approach. Because information about ASIST has not yet been published, this chapter will not give details of the method.

In ASIST, with the therapist's direction, the client develops a question for which he or she does not have a conscious answer. Mentally, the client goes to his or her own personal paradise, gathers three helpers, and seeks answers to the question.

My first ASIST was incredible. I asked why I kept getting into difficulties at work and received the initial answer "Because you need to." I thought, So tell me something I don't know.

In my visualization at the time I received this message, I had been transported from my personal paradise, on my beach in Maui, to the top of a waterfall in Hawaii. I, who do not like heights and cannot swim, then jumped from the top of the waterfall into a whirlpool, where I kept going around and around, aware of people assembled on the periphery. In my meditative state I eventually thought, It's boring just going around in circles. As I thought this, I was transported out the bottom of the whirlpool and onto a glassy indigo-blue stream.

Earlier that morning, I had been looking at a painting that I like in the cancer clinic. The painting is of sunflowers and had an indigo-blue background. In my visualization, wisps of gold started coming from the sides of the blue stream. I understood that things were beginning to change and that the wisps of gold would eventually become the beautiful yellow sunflowers. I asked, Who might help me on my journey? I received the message that my oncologist, two primary nurses, and an administrator would be helpful. The first three had already saved my life, so I guess they had helped. I thought the message about the administrator was strange, but two days later she called. She said she recognized that I was not happy in my job and perhaps we should meet to discuss this.

As I did ASIST, I found things unfolding for me. I began to refer clients to Dr. Rossiter-Thornton so they also could gain new insights. One of these people found a book on prayer and discovered that she could get the same answers praying that she could through doing ASIST. This led Dr. Rossiter-Thornton to develop the Prayer Wheel (Rossiter-Thornton, 2000), a nondenominational model for praying in which one connects with a source of healing: the collective unconscious, one's higher self, the Maker of Life, God, Buddah, or Allah (see Figure 2-1).

In the Listen section of the wheel, "people often record very specific thoughts, directives, or guidance, frequently in a style different from their own" (Rossiter-Thornton, 2000, p. 126). At the least, regular use of the Prayer Wheel provides a sense of peace; some people receive guidance that can be of great benefit in life.

As I began to use the Prayer Wheel, I found that I was connecting to God in a way that I had not previously experienced. I received direction on my path, advice about how to handle situations, warnings about health issues, and reprimands when I wasn't doing things the way I might. Generally, I felt connected with "someone" who saw the bigger picture of my life. The language of the directives and warnings I received was not in the style I usually use, and biblical phrases, which I never would spontaneously use, were interspersed throughout.

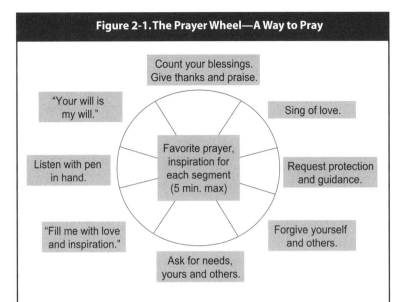

Figure 2-1. The Prayer Wheel—A Way to Pray

Prayer is a self-help technique that costs nothing, requires no equipment, and can be used in any situation. The Prayer Wheel can be used by anyone, regardless of background, belief, religion, or race.

Starting at the top, going clockwise, use your favorite inspirational stories, songs, poems, or prayers to follow the instructions shown for each segment of the wheel. For example, in the "Sing" segment, sing your favorite love songs to the Maker of Life. In the "Ask" segment, record and date your requests. In the "Listen" segment, simply sit quietly and listen. Should any thoughts, words, or ideas come to your mind at this time, write them down and date them.

The wheel takes 40 minutes, using 5 minutes per segment. If you have less time, either shorten the segments or just complete the segments you most need. Do not shorten the Listen segment, however.

You don't have to believe in prayer for it to be spiritually beneficial; just pray with love in your heart.

Note. Figure copyright © 2000 by Rossiter-Thornton Associates. Used with permission.

I began to suggest that my clients use the Prayer Wheel, and many did. Some received guidance; others found their prayers being answered. A woman who was just beginning to have a spiritual connection for the first time prayed to have some real contact with her mother, who had been schizophrenic since my client was 10 years old. Within a few weeks, she had her first real conversation with her mother, who soon reverted to her schizophrenic form of communication. A Muslim woman with advanced cancer prayed for healing in her relationship with her husband, help for his depression, and help with their financial problems. He was totally unaware that she was praying for these things. Within a few days he invited her to come to his therapist with him, and they achieved a major breakthrough in their communication. He started on antidepressants, his depression began to lift, and he was offered a job at twice his salary. A few weeks later, as she entered the final stage of her illness, he said to me, "I don't know what you are doing with my wife, but I have the woman back that I married and that I haven't seen for the past two years." My response was that *I* wasn't doing anything; she was being helped through her prayers.

CASE STUDY 2: BOB

Bob was a 34-year-old very successful businessman who was referred to me because of stage II lymphoma. He was then receiving third-line chemotherapy with the hope of getting him into remission so that he could have a stem cell transplant. Bob had spoken with a psychiatrist and expressed the wish to work with someone who could integrate spirituality into psychotherapy. Bob had never been a spiritual person, but he had read that people with a spiritual outlook did better than others in fighting disease. Bob took this quite seriously. He made contact with the minister who had married him and his wife a couple of years previously. He did some serious reflecting regarding himself, his relationships, and his life, with the goal of healing what needed to be healed. He began to meet regularly with the minister as well as me, whom he chose as his psychotherapist.

When Bob was referred to me, he was in the hospital and having severe difficulty swallowing secondary to an esophageal ulcer associated with chemotherapy. In his first session of ASIST, he asked how he could get through the next two chemotherapy treatments in order to heal. After connecting with his three helpers and before starting his first ASIST journey, Bob received advice from his helpers: "Be strong and have faith."

In ASIST, the identified helpers take the person to the places in the nonconscious mind where they can find the answers that they need. His helper who was the primary spokesperson for the first journey was the chef Emeril Lagasse. Bob was taken to Emeril's kitchen, where he was told that he had to "start eating, be brave, try things, don't get discouraged." He was told that he could avoid getting discouraged through "patience, trust, and trust in his doctors." When his guide was asked if there were particular things that Bob should be eating, Bob was told, "Soup. Start slowly. Chicken noodle, cream of mushroom." Over the next couple of sessions, Bob spoke about the chicken noodle and mushroom soup that he was having, but he had no memory of having been advised to eat these foods. His esophageal ulcer became less troublesome, and he did not have the same ulcer problem in his next course of chemotherapy.

Over time, Bob reported that he was accepting of death but hoping to stay alive. Bob used the Prayer Wheel on occasion. The second meditation we did was one in which Bob asked, "Where can I find the strength to get through the next eight days of chemotherapy, physically, mentally, and spiritually?" The dialog that follows chronicles my interaction with Bob as we worked through the Listen section of the Prayer Wheel.

Bob: I have an image of being held by God. It's a typical image of God: long hair, beard, and long robe. He is holding somebody. I can't make out that it's me, but I know that it's me.

I feel incredibly heavy right now. I'm scared. I'm comforted by being held and know that, if I do die, I'll be in God's kingdom. I'll be comforted. I'm scared that, if I do die, I don't get to spend any more time with [my wife].

I get the feeling that I'm doing the right thing. I have no indication of whether I'll live or die, but that I'm doing the right thing.

Everything's dark. I'm still being held. I think that the reason why my paradise is the way it is [a beautiful room with an ocean view, with wife, family of origin, in-laws, lots of food and drink, and a hockey rink that is near a golf course] is that I don't want to let go of this dimension. I'm not ready to let go of this dimension. I want my family to be with me in my paradise. I'm scared of not being with them.

MV: Lord, how can you help Bob with the feelings that he is having?

Bob: I'm getting a feeling that my faith isn't strong enough yet. I feel that it is getting a bit lighter now. I need to work on my faith.

MV: How can he work on his faith during these eight days?

Bob: I'm hearing "Trust me." I'm hearing "I'm always with you."

A few days later, Bob did a meditation in which he asked, "What can I do to get closer to God and thus facilitate my healing?" That meditation developed like this:

Bob: I need to be more thankful for all the blessings that He has given me. I need to appreciate these blessings, not just the obvious ones–try to discern the ones that are not so obvious.

I have to truly believe . . . that . . . no matter what the outcome is of my illness, that it was . . . what was best for me.

[I] need to let go–I'm not sure of what–just let go and trust in the journey that God is taking me on.

He says that He knows that I'm trying because He knows that I believe in Him, that I love Him. Just got to let go.

MV: Are there other words that Bob needs to hear before we finish?

Bob: Just that He loves me. He's with me.

Bob found the imagery of God holding him to be very powerful and helpful, and he used it to help him to fall asleep. He found that his sleeping improved considerably by using this image. In addition, he was able to feel God's hand reaching into the left side of his chest and bringing comfort to the area of his largest tumor.

In mid-January, I had a dream in which a young patient, Walter, who had died of leukemia at age 34, appeared. In my dream, I asked what he had come for. Walter said that he had come to help Bob.

At about the same time, Bob had a dream in which he saw himself dying and going to the next world. He looked down and saw his wife crying at his bedside. He returned to be with her.

We discussed these dreams. Bob asked if I thought that Walter had come to help him to live or to die. I said that I assumed that Walter had come to help him to live. Bob felt encouraged because of his dream of seeing himself come back from death.

One week later, it became obvious that Bob's disease was rapidly progressing. He would not be able to have a stem cell transplant, and he would soon die. He and his wife accepted this with great equanimity and returned home to spend their final weeks together, with their family and friends. Bob received palliative care during this time, and his oncologist visited to help with symptom relief.

On February 12, Bob asked his wife if it was Valentine's Day. She said it wasn't and asked why he was asking. He replied that Valentine's Day would be a beautiful day to die.

I saw Bob the next day, and he said, "Someone is dying and it isn't me." I assured him that, in dying, he would not really die; he would have everlasting life. He repeated that someone was dying and it wasn't him; it might not even be someone that he knew. It appeared that Bob was in the space between living and dying, where people sometimes experience special visions.

The next day, Valentine's Day, another client who had been doing spiritual work died (Vachon & Shaver, in press).

Bob said that he could not die until I had met his parents. We met on February 15, and Bob died peacefully on February 16.

CANCER AS A SPIRITUALLY TRANSFORMING EXPERIENCE

In her work, Yvonne Kason, MD–a Toronto family practitioner, psychotherapist, and mystic–wrote about STEs. "STEs are part of a transformation and expansion of consciousness in which we become intermittently capable of perceiving other levels of reality, including what we might consider mystical or paranormal dimensions. STEs appear to be signs that this transformation may be accelerating" (Kason, 2000, pp. 20–21). Kason explained that STEs include
• Mystical experiences
• Psychic awakening
• Near-death experiences
• Spontaneously inspired creativity and genius

- Episodes of spiritual energy, or kundalini
- Spiritual energy cross-culturally, or the ability to be in touch with people from other cultures while in a meditative state.

In mystical experiences, one experiences transcendence of the self and union with the divine (Kason, 2000). Bob of Case Study 2 had such a strong mystical experience that its impact stayed with him until the end of his life. These experiences are happening to many average people (Kason). In referring to the work of psychologist William James, Yvonne Kason listed four characteristics of mystical experiences. Ineffably, mystical experiences

1. Defy expression. It is essentially impossible for the experiencer to convey their importance, grandeur, or profundity to another. They have to be experienced to be fully comprehended.
2. Have a noetic, or intellectual, component. Although mystical experiences are similar to states of feeling, they also are states of knowing. The experience contains revelations, illuminations, and insights into depths of truth.
3. Are transient. Except in rare cases, mystical experiences cannot be sustained for long, although they may bring about a continual development in inner richness in those who experience them.
4. Engender passivity. Although certain practices may facilitate a mystical state, after the state has begun, "the mystic feels as if his own will were in abeyance [or] . . . as if he were grasped and held by a superior power" (Kason, 2000, p. 33).

People who are being transformed will find that their lives have a more spiritual focus, that their sense of connection to a loving Higher Power deepens, and that they have much stronger ethical convictions and a stronger need to embrace personal emotional healing and recovery (Kason, 2000).

As my life has been changing, I try to start each morning with qi gong and prayer, including the Serenity Prayer and the Prayer of St. Francis ("Lord, make me an instrument of thy peace"). I repeat a phrase that was given to someone doing ASIST: Dr. Rossiter-Thornton uses the acronym "lga fitwog"–Let go and float in the will of God. In addition, I have begun to use the Grace Prayer of the Unity Church: "Please heal in me what needs to be healed. Please teach me what I need to learn. I surrender my life to you. Thy will be done" (Kason, 2000, p. 284).

THE IMPACT OF SPIRITUALITY ON MY CLINICAL WORK

As my life has unfolded in unexpected directions, my work with clients has changed. As part of my initial assessment of a client, I now ask whether spirituality is a part of his or her life and whether the client uses it to cope with illness or bereavement. If a client has an interest in spirituality, I mention that research has affirmed that spirituality can be helpful in coping with life crises and transitions (Dossey, 1996; Sulmasy, 1997). I state that my own journey with cancer has led to an increased awareness of spirituality and mention the Prayer Wheel and ASIST (Vachon, 2000). (Between half and two-thirds of the people I am currently seeing are exploring spiritual issues and using the Prayer Wheel and ASIST.) In addition, we discuss the client's adjustment to illness and bereavement, problems and symptoms, coping techniques the client is using and others that might be helpful, and various complementary approaches.

As clients use spiritual or meditative practices, they often feel a peace and calmness in dealing with their illnesses—not all the time, but more often than before using these practices. Many have begun to pray and to integrate other practices (e.g., yoga, meditation, qi gong, touch therapies) into their lives as they deal with illness or bereavement. Many of my clients find that their spiritual and complementary practices make dealing with the issues that confront them easier, and this is what matters most.

IMPLICATIONS FOR ONCOLOGY NURSES

Oncology nurses who are interested in integrating the Prayer Wheel, meditation, or other spiritual channels of healing into their clinical practice should first reflect on how spirituality is integrated into their own lives. It also is crucial that the nurse not seek to proselytize, or try to convert patients to a particular way of thinking or believing. He or she must raise the issue of spirituality with clients in a nonintrusive way. The nurse should offer to meditate, do guided visualization, pray, or use tools such as the Prayer Wheel with the patient if, and only if, the patient is interested in such approaches. Because many people are uncomfortable discussing matters of prayer and spirituality initially, the nurse should offer these resources again as rapport develops and if the nurse is comfortable with these issues.

Nurses using spiritual techniques with patients should have someone trained in spiritual counseling or meditation as a supervisor or consultant. Chaplains, pastoral counselors, or clergy of the patient's faith can be of great help, and nurses must refer to these resources or to psychiatry, psychology, or mental health staff in regard to issues that the nurse is unequipped to handle.

Research is showing that patients are interested in exploring their spirituality with clinicians (Ehman, Ott, Short, Ciampa, & Hansen-Flaschen, 1999). In a study of Canadian patients with cancer (N = 1,414), 40% used prayer, 20% used exercise, 19% relaxed via stress management, and 12% used a special diet as a response to their illness. These approaches were used for anxiety reduction (42%), to improve quality of life (29%), to influence the course of disease (28%), and to improve the patient's sense of control (24%) (Vachon, Fitch, Greenberg, & Franssen, 1994; Vachon, Lancee, Conway, & Adair, 1990; Vachon, Lancee, Ghadirian, Adair, & Conway, 1991). In a study of 45 terminally ill patients, 69% used spiritual approaches (Connolly et al., 2002). Furthermore, remarkable recoveries have been associated with spiritual transformation (Hirshberg & Barasch, 1995). As nurses committed to providing holistic care, we are obligated to improve our ability to tap into a patient's own spiritual source of strength and healing.

REFERENCES

Connolly, R., Vachon, M., Hollenberg, D., Librach, L., Chow, E., Danjoux, C., et al. (2002). *The use of complementary and alternative therapies among patients referred to an outpatient palliative radiotherapy programme.* Unpublished manuscript.

Dossey, L. (1996). *Prayer is good medicine: How to reap the healing benefits of prayer.* San Francisco: HarperSanFrancisco.

Ehman, J.W., Ott, B.B., Short, T.H., Ciampa, R.C., & Hansen-Flaschen, J. (1999). Do patients want physicians to inquire about their spiritual or religious beliefs if they become gravely ill? *Archives of Internal Medicine, 23,* 1803–1806.

Hirshberg, C., & Barasch, M.I. (1995). *Remarkable recovery.* New York: Riverhead Books.

Kason, Y. (2000). *Farther shores: Exploring how near-death, kundalini, and other mystical experiences can transform ordinary lives.* Toronto: HarperCollinsCanada.

Kearney, M. (1996). *Mortally wounded: Stories of soul pain, death, and healing.* New York: Scribner.

Pope, R. (1991). *Illness and healing: Images of cancer.* Hantsport, Nova Scotia: Lancelot Press.

Rossiter-Thornton, J.F. (2000). Prayer in psychotherapy. *Alternative Therapies, 6*(1), 125–127.

Schultz, M.L. (1998). *Awakening intuition.* New York: Harmony Books.

Sulmasy, D.P. (1997). *The healer's calling.* New York: Paulist Press.

Underwood, M. (1995). *Diary of a death professional.* Hartford, CT: Association for Death Education and Counseling.

Vachon, M.L.S. (2000). Live and learn: Cancer as a transformational experience. *The Forum Newsletter, 26*(2), 5–6.

Vachon, M.L.S., Fitch, M., Greenberg, M., & Franssen, E. (1994). [The needs of persons living with cancer.] Unpublished raw data.

Vachon, M.L.S., Lancee, W.J., Conway, B., & Adair, W.K. (1990). *The needs of persons living with cancer in Manitoba.* Toronto: Canadian Cancer Society.

Vachon, M.L.S., Lancee, W.J., Ghadirian, P., Adair, W.K., & Conway, B. (1991). *Report on the needs of persons living with cancer in Quebec.* Toronto: Canadian Cancer Society.

Vachon, M.L.S., & Shaver, W.A. (in press). Suffering in the face of terminal illness. In R. Sunlop, C. Davis, N. Coyle, & R. Portenoy (Eds.), *Concise Oxford textbook of palliative care.* Oxford, England: Oxford Medical Publications.

Chapter 3

Scripts for Guided Imagery

Scripts for Guided Imagery

Denise Murray Edwards, RN, CS, ARNP, MA, MEd, MTS

Imagery is a powerful lever to move the mind-body world for others and ourselves. Some people seem to always have known this and used imagery. Others act as if they had no control over their imagining.

The images that we all have in our memory and the imagery that, consciously and unconsciously, is ongoing in our minds are products of our personality and experience. They are fed by what we have witnessed, heard about, seen in movies or television, imagined, composed from other images, and created in our dreams. The sum of this imagery as it is going on would tell us much about who and what we are at any given moment. And yet, imagery is both cause and effect. We are its product no more than it is ours. We can and do choose—at least part of the time—what new material to add to the mix and determine what we want to "image" (imagine). How we make these choices can affect our mental and physical states so significantly that some people can have surgery under hypnosis, which is a type of focused imagining, rather than an anesthetic. It is little wonder that imagery has been used to decrease pain, anxiety, nausea, and insomnia.

A script for guided imagery consists of directions that allow the listener to activate his or her own imagination in a way that appeals to the senses, distracts the listener from stressful stimuli, and connects the listener with concepts that may be helpful. This chapter will present guidelines for creating scripts and a sampling of scripts by different authors. Discussion and scripts are grouped according to the symptom the imagery is designed to address.

You might begin your experience of imagery by incorporating it into your own self-care. How surprised you will be at the level of relaxation you can achieve by creating images with and for your powerful mind.

THE NEED FOR IMAGERY TO APPEAL TO THE SENSES

Imagery scripts include directions to use sense memories to create a deep and rich image that replaces the surface content of the mind. The holistic premise is that two things cannot occupy the same "space." Often, when a person is ill and perhaps afraid, empty time quickly fills with worries. Instead, imagery can fill that space. The most effective scripts interlace images that appeal to various senses, eliciting them alternately, then together. It is the weaving together of sensory images that creates the compelling quality of the imagery, allowing the images to occupy the inner space and displace fear, tension, and worry.

Creating Visual Images

The first task usually is to set the scene. Being vague when doing this may be helpful. By being vague, you allow the listener to fill in the specific content; your words will not clash with the image already being created from the listener's personal store of images.

Consider this scene-setting example from a guided imagery script:

> With your mind's eye, I'd like you to see yourself lying on a comfortable wooden raft, close to the shore on a gentle body of water on a warm day.

This simple direction contains many ideas. The raft is wooden, so to most people it will seem safe. It is placed close to the shore for the same reason. Occasionally, after completing this imagery, clients tell me that they are afraid of the water, so they placed the raft in a swimming pool. Others convert the surface of the raft to soft plastic. Even during explicit description, some patients instinctively change your words to increase their relaxation. The day is described as warm to promote relaxation but is not described as sunny, because many treatments and medications make sun exposure a problem. You could substitute other words that connote less heat (e.g., *balmy*); however, at this point, you are already interweaving another sensory modality. Note that the "sense" of emotional states is commonly attended to as in *safe, calm, relaxed, or remembered wellness.* Images are chosen to promote states of emotional well-being. The sense of being relaxed or safe is best understood as a kinesthetic or proprioceptive experience or memory.

Sometimes, a client has difficulty creating visual images. In this instance, an introduction that relies on "word images" may be helpful. Word images derive from visualizing the process of one's life, noticing the flow and rhythm of this unique journey. Marsha Hines, MA, developed the following elegant word image.

> Life unfolds, as we learn, in the most unexpected and mysterious way as we mature. In our younger days, we set our goals, mapped out our life on a piece of paper as if it were a 100-piece puzzle that we could simply sit down one afternoon and put together. There is most definitely a plan, but not according to our timetable or control. We take the inevitable twists and turns on our life path, but not until we reach a certain delicate point in our life do we see (if we're lucky) the synchronicity of events and people in our lives and how beautifully it develops without our manipulation and control, usually by letting go and effortlessly just letting it happen . . . and trusting—in ourselves, other human beings, and other phenomena that occur if we can but be still and listen.

The last script in this chapter, "Numbers," by Warren P. Edwards, PhD, also may be effective with clients who find imagining visual images difficult.

Creating Auditory Images

The task is to invite the recipient to hear relaxing sounds that are consistent with the visual imagery. Repetition often is helpful. For example,

> As you lie there, with nothing to do but feel comfortable and feel relaxed, you may be able to hear sounds from the shore or from the air—perhaps the sound that water makes as it gently splashes against a wooden surface, a rhythmic sound, a restful sound.

Use of the word "may" in the construction of the image gives *permission* but does not make *demands*. It is important that the recipient does not have performance anxiety or feel a sense of failure when a part of the directed image does not occur.

Creating Kinesthetic Images

The kinesthetic piece of the image involves movement, position, or tactile or thermal sensation. The passive imagery that follows emphasizes sensation.

As you rest there, listening to the sounds from the water, from the air, from the shore, you may or you may not be able to feel the gentle warmth of the sun as it shines on you and warms the wooden raft beneath you. You might be able to feel the support of the raft underneath your head, your shoulders, your back, your hips, your legs, as you rest there with nothing to do but feel peaceful, feel relaxed.

Again, the language gives the listener permission to have an experience that is different from the one the guide is describing. It may facilitate relaxation, to begin by overlapping the senses at this point.

Directions, such as "feel the support," need to be roughly congruent with actual position and, when possible, tactile cues (e.g., the client listening to the preceding imagery should actually be positioned against some support, such as a bed or recliner chair).

Creating Images That Appeal to Multiple Senses

The imagery scripts that seem most effective create complex images that appeal to multiple senses simultaneously. The imagery that follows evokes several senses, including the "sense" of humor.

You may notice clouds in the sky above you, noticing the color of the sky, seeing the edges of the clouds where they are thin and you can see through them to the color of the sky, noticing the centers of the clouds where they are thick like cotton. You may or you may not be able to see shapes in the clouds, perhaps familiar

> shapes or amusing shapes or shapes you have never seen before, perhaps feeling the movement of the breeze on your face as it moves the clouds across the surface of the sky.

Clients often find multisensory imagery so relaxing that they fall asleep. This is especially likely if the client is in bed. In my experience, if left undisturbed, a client will sleep for about four hours after guided imagery.

There is a hypnogogic phase of early sleep. Noise, in the early stages of sleep, can not only shatter the sleep state but also can create stress. Think of your own experience of the telephone ringing as you are falling asleep. You probably felt startled and, perhaps, disoriented. To protect a client from this, stay with him or her for approximately five minutes after the client seems to have fallen asleep. Monitor the environment by answering the telephone or diverting anyone who comes to see the patient. When I leave a client, my habit is to touch the client's hand gently and say that I am leaving. I encourage the client to slip into a deeper sleep. To sleep well, it is important to feel safe.

SAMPLE SCRIPTS

Guided imagery can be easily modified to adjust to changing needs. Clinicians with a wide range of training and experience have developed and used the scripts that appear in this chapter. After the first script, whose purpose is to help the client become centered (i.e., mindful, grounded in the moment, receptive to imagery), the scripts are clustered according to the symptom they are designed to help manage. All the scripts can be used simply for relaxation and distraction from pain. Feel free to use these scripts, modify them, or create your own. Some scripts include the direction to include music. A wide variety of relaxing music is available (see Chapter 4). You can experiment with sounds that you and your client find enhance the message of the guided image.

You will develop a sense of timing by watching clients. You can begin by pacing your voice to the speed of their breathing and gradually slowing your pace, leading them to the relaxation response.

Technique for Centering Prior to Healing Work

Gloria Green, RN, OCN®

This script is best delivered with the client in a supine position, but it can be effective regardless of the client's position. This script calls for you to touch the client. Your hands must be warm. My experience is that people with cold hands may be unaware of that fact. So I recommend that all practitioners warm their hands under warm water before delivering this imagery.

[Gently cup the back of the patient's neck with the palm of one hand. You will find through experience which hand is most comfortable for you to use. When your hand is in place, say this slowly:]

_____ *[say the client's name]*, feel this hand on the back of your neck and think of it as a gate that is closing on the past: past moments, past hours, past days, past weeks. Let the past—with its worries, fears, anxieties, and all the good times as well—drop away and bring your mind softly into the present moment, free and unencumbered by that past. It is all behind the gate, behind my hand.

[Now place your other hand, palm down, on the patient's forehead and say this:]

I take my other hand and place it on your forehead, _____ *[say the client's name]*, and I want you to think of it as a gate that is closing on the future. It is our human nature to run to the future in our minds and imagine what we think the future holds for us. The future is not ours to know, so there is no need to go there right now. Instead, let your mind settle into the present moment, _____ *[say the client's name]*, in the now time, the only time any of us really has. Allow yourself the luxury of being relaxed and fully focused, here and now, in this special time for healing that we have been given to share with each other. No past. No future. Just now. If you find thoughts coming in, just let them come and watch them go, without attachment. Your task here is to do . . . nothing.

Scripts to Displace Nausea

Most of us, in our experience of nausea, have had the thought that we would feel better with some fresh air. Often, introducing the image of a cooling breeze can bring back a sense of well-being.

Finding Peace

Mary Joan Meyer, FSM

> Make yourself comfortable in your chair or bed. Keep your arms and legs relaxed. Don't cross your legs. Close your eyes. Become completely still.
>
> Be aware of your breathing. Breathe in and breathe out.
>
> Let go of tensions. Feel the air as it moves in and out of your nostrils. Inhale and exhale slowly, allowing yourself to become completely relaxed.
>
> Listen to the music and try to clear your mind of all thoughts. Imagine yourself out in the country on a bright day.
>
> The sky is beautiful, deep blue. Puffy clouds are scattered across the sky. There is a cool breeze. You are very comfortable.
>
> There is a dirt road near you, one with grass and weeds on both sides. Start walking along the road. Be aware of the noises of insects, small animals, and birds. There's a bend in the road.
>
> When you go around it, you see a big oak tree on a mound overlooking the valley. Sit under the tree and look out over the valley. Or lie down on the grass and look at the sky, if you wish. Just relax and be at peace. This is your time. Enjoy it.
>
> I will tell you when it's time to come back home.

To Jennifer, My Gift to You

Joann Sanders, RNC, MS, CHTP

The imagery in this script expands on the theme of the healing power of nature. It is more complex than the preceding script, and the images change frequently, involving movement. Notice the dream-like quality of the travel, which occurs instantly and yet is easily accepted. You will see complexity and dreamlike travel combined again, later in this chapter, in the script titled "Brookside."

Make yourself comfortable. Put both feet on the floor, your hands in your lap or at your side. Close your eyes. Allow yourself to become . . . calm . . . and quiet.

Breathe naturally. As you inhale, say to yourself . . . I am. As you exhale, say . . . relaxed. I am . . . relaxed. I am . . . relaxed.

Are there any . . . environmental sounds that distract you? Listen to them. Let them fade away. Such noises do not need your attention.

If you feel any tension, consciously let it go. Replace it with: I am . . . relaxed.

Today, take your mind . . . and imagination . . . away from here. Go to a comfortable place. _____ *[say the client's name],* picture, at a distance, an inviting beach. Let the beach be like a landscape: seen hazily from afar . . . becoming clearer and clearer as you approach it.

As you approach, slip off your shoes. Feel the warm sand . . . under your feet . . . and between your toes. Feel how it trickles through your toes.

Sit down. Be relaxed . . . and comfortable. The sun is bright, creating shadows on the sand. Maybe a few clouds roll by, obscuring the sun's warmth momentarily. You can feel . . . a light breeze cooling your body.

Take a deep breath . . . and give yourself over to the sun . . . and the fresh air. Feel the peace . . . that surrounds you. Slowly get up . . . and walk toward the water.

Look out at the water. Its blue blends with the blue horizon.

Before you know it, your feet feel the sand becoming a little cooler and damp. Soon you find you are splashing in ankle-deep water. The water is a cool relief from the hot sand, but the water is actually quite warm.

Now sit down in the wet sand. Stretch out your legs before you. Watch the waves. They are small and breaking softly. Feel the peace . . . that surrounds you. You become more and more relaxed.

You begin to explore . . . things in your life. Allow your fears . . . your anxieties . . . to easily fade, becoming aware of your inner peace.

Refill yourself with new ideas, new awareness, new experiences, and new relationships.

Lean back, slowly allowing your body to lie flat on the wet sand. Listen as the small waves break. Feel the water that gently surrounds you. It remains shallow, no deeper than a couple of inches.

Feel the water ebb away. Feel the sun, warm on your body. Look up at the blue sky. You are feeling very relaxed, enjoying the warmth from the sun. Your body is wrapped in warmth. You are feeling very safe.

As you look around . . . you see someone.

It is your guide, St. Gabriel the Archangel. He appears to be asking you . . . to follow.

You soon find yourself in front of a stately old mansion.

You feel very drawn to it. It seems well cared for. It seems to sparkle.

You walk up the steps that lead to the entrance. You soon find yourself in front of a beautiful paneled door. You lift the ornate brass knocker. Soon the door is opened. You are greeted by an old friend . . . someone you haven't thought of in years. You are both happy to see each other. Your friend invites you into the mansion.

You see a beautiful room, with white carpet–thick white carpet. The room is filled with fluffy pillows. You find yourself sitting on the carpeted floor. You feel contentment to be surrounded by such beauty and comfort.

You are very relaxed, feeling the peace and healing within you.

There is a soft breeze coming in an open window. This breeze is the movement of your life. It comes . . . and goes . . . in cycles, yet always in a direction . . . toward healing.

You may become aware of thoughts and feelings that have been moving about . . . back and forth . . . in your mind. Be aware of these thoughts . . . of these feelings. Let them come to rest in the inner peace of your mind. Let any negative thoughts or feelings float away with the wind.

Your mind becomes more and more at rest. Your feelings become more and more serene. Your body becomes more and more calm. This is your time for inner healing.

The wind gives you energy for healing. It gives you peace and serenity. You feel light. Relaxed. At peace.

This is a spot to return to whenever you need to relax or find inner peace. This is a safe place to be.

You feel better than you did before we started. And you are ready to return to today. I'll count to five. At five, you will slowly open your eyes.

One: You are beginning to return.

Two, three: Your body is feeling calm.

Four and five: Your mind is clear and alert.

Slowly open your eyes to let in the light.

Scripts to Displace Insomnia

Difficulty falling and staying asleep is a common problem among patients with cancer. Sleep problems are particularly troublesome during periods of hospitalization. Several years ago, when working at the Dana-Farber Cancer Institute in Boston, my colleagues and I developed a video for staff and patients to learn about complementary interventions for pain and anxiety. One day, a frustrated student nurse took the manual that accompanied the video and simply read the relaxation script to a patient who could not fall asleep. Because she had never read the material before, the nurse's eyes were glued to the page. How surprised she was to look up and see the patient sleeping soundly! What a wonderful experience for both of them.

Combining Relaxation, Rhythmic Breathing, and Imagery

Judith A. Spross, PhD, RN

In this script, note how breathing exercises, autogenic relaxation instructions, and guided imagery blend for the purpose of easing tension and wakefulness.

Get into a comfortable position, lying or sitting. Arms should be at your sides or, if you're sitting, in your lap. Legs should be uncrossed. Let your jaw drop to relax your facial muscles.

I'd like you to begin by taking some deep, slow, cleansing breaths. Breathe in . . . breathe out. I'd like you to think about your hands. Feel your hands becoming warm, heavy, and relaxed as you breathe in slowly and deeply . . . and exhale slowly. Breathe in . . . breathe out. In . . . out.

Feel the warmth and relaxation flow from your hands into the muscles of your forearms and upper arms. Feel those muscles become warm, heavy, and relaxed as you breathe in slowly and deeply. Breathe in . . . breathe out. In . . . out. Your hands and arms feel warm, heavy, and relaxed.

Now feel the warmth and relaxation flow from your arms into the muscles of your shoulders, neck, and head. Feel these muscles become warm, heavy, and relaxed as you breathe in slowly and deeply . . . and exhale slowly. Breathe in . . . breathe out. Breathe in warmth and relaxation; breathe out tension and pain. The muscles of your head, neck, and shoulders feel warm, heavy, and relaxed.

Feel the warmth and relaxation flow from the muscles of your arms, shoulders, neck, and head into the muscles of your upper back and chest. Feel these muscles become warm, heavy, and relaxed as you breathe in slowly and deeply . . . and exhale slowly. Breathe in . . . breathe out. The muscles of your chest and upper back feel warm, heavy, and relaxed.

Now feel the warmth and relaxation flow from your chest and upper back into the muscles of your abdomen and lower back. Feel these muscles become warm, heavy, and relaxed as you breathe in slowly and deeply . . . and exhale slowly. Breathe in . . . breathe out. The muscles of your abdomen feel warm, heavy, and relaxed.

Now feel the warmth and relaxation flow into the muscles of your pelvis and buttocks. Feel these muscles become warm, heavy, and relaxed as you breathe in slowly and deeply . . . and exhale slowly. Breathe in . . . breathe out. The muscles of your pelvis and buttocks feel warm, heavy, and relaxed.

Now feel the warmth and relaxation flow into the muscles of your legs and feet. Feel these muscles become warm, heavy, and relaxed as you breathe in slowly and deeply . . . and exhale slowly. Breathe in . . . breathe out. The muscles of your legs and feet feel warm, heavy, and relaxed.

I'd like you to be aware, now, that your whole body is totally relaxed. You feel warm, relaxed, and comfortable. Continue breathing in and out, slowly and deeply. And, while you are feeling relaxed, I'd like you to imagine that your eyelids are a movie screen. See yourself in that special place, the place where you usually feel relaxed and comfortable. It may be indoors or outdoors; you may be alone or with others. Use all your senses to enter this place of peace, comfort, and relaxation. Be aware of what you see. Be aware of what you feel. Are you warm or cool? Be aware of the aromas, the smells, associated with this special place. Think about what you hear. Hear those sounds now. You are in your special place, feeling comfortable and relaxed. Spend some time there, enjoying this time away.

[Allow 1 minute or more to elapse, then continue.]

At the count of three, take a deep breath, let it out slowly, and open your eyes. When you open your eyes, you will feel alert, relaxed, and comfortable.

[This last instruction can be modified for subsequent coaching sessions or for an individualized cassette by offering the client the option of remaining relaxed with eyes closed but advising the client that your coaching will end.]

Cleansing and Energizing

Denise Murray Edwards, RN, ARNP, MA, MEd, MTS

The next script was developed for a client who was experiencing severe anxiety. She had been diagnosed with carpal tunnel syndrome when, in fact, she had lung cancer that had metastasized to her brain. I began the imagery session by using Healing Touch followed by

"Cleansing and Energizing." The combination enabled her to relax enough to sleep. The client used a tape of this imagery every afternoon to prepare for a nap.

Make yourself comfortable. You may be in a chair, or in bed, or on the floor. Begin to feel your body slowing down, your breathing slowing down. Just listen to my words because I will tell you what to do every step of the way.

With your mind's eye, imagine a ball of energy hovering over the surface of your abdomen, also called the lower *dan tien*. Notice any colors or textures or movement in your ball of energy.

Now imagine that you have lifted it up above the crown of your head. Hold it there briefly, and begin to move this ball of energy into your head. Move it down through your head, neck, chest, and, finally, settle it in your abdomen, your lower *dan tien*.

Now, using your mind's eye, imagine that a stream of healing energy is flowing from that ball of energy; moving toward your right hip; bathing the bones, muscles, and sinews with its healing energy. Cleansing any debris left from movement or pain or fatigue, and pushing that debris forward toward the right foot as the stream continues its journey, cleansing the areas of the upper right thigh, moving toward the knee, bringing light and warmth into any dark place. Cleansing. Nurturing. Nourishing the structures and tissues as it continues its journey toward the right calf. Renewing the tissues with its healing, cleansing energy. Moving the debris forward toward the right foot. Bathing the joint of the right ankle. Nurturing and nourishing the tissues as it moves forward, bathing the right foot. Bringing light to any dark place. Cleansing the bones, muscles, and sinews of the right foot, and pushing forward all the debris into the universe to be renewed and cleansed until it again becomes positive energy.

And now, if you'll direct your attention again to the ball of energy in your abdomen: The stream of healing energy moves from the ball toward your left hip, bathing the structures, nurturing and nourishing the tissues as it cleanses any debris from this area. Moving forward toward the left thigh, it brings light to any areas needing special attention, moving to the knee as you direct your attention, as best you can, to the healing of this one area of your body, your left knee. Note feelings of relaxation as the energy bathes your left calf in its healing warmth, cleansing any debris from this area. The energy that you see with your mind's eye moves forward to your left ankle and foot, filling the area with warm, healing energy and moving any waste into the universe to be recycled.

Again, you may return your attention to the ball of your energy in your abdomen. A stream moves upward, bathing your organs of reproduction, your bladder, kidneys, spleen–all the contents of your abdomen receive this cleansing, energizing attention as it continues on its way upward. The energy bathes your lungs, your heart, thanking them for their work in maintaining your body. The energy cleanses them and surrounds them with healing warmth. The energy continues on its way, dividing at your neck and flowing down both arms, surrounding your shoulders, upper arms, and elbows. It moves forward any debris from the work of your arms, moving gently around the muscles and joints, nurturing and nourishing. The energy moves that debris out through your fingers into the universe to be cleansed.

[You may choose to relax each arm separately.]

Finally, move your attention to your neck as the energy moves upward through your head, bathing this important area of your body with its healing warmth, as you direct your attention as best you can to your wonderful brain. The energy moves any residue forward and out through your crown, to be cleansed in the universe.

And now, move your mind through your body to discover if any part needs a little extra attention today. If there are such places, direct some extra love and energy to these areas.

[*You may pause for 1 to 2 minutes.*]

And now that you have cleansed your body and filled it with healing energy, you may take this renewed energy and reorient yourself to your breathing and your place in this room. Or you may continue to rest and, if you choose, drift off to sleep. . . .

Scripts to Displace Anxiety

Anxiety can prevent a client from focusing on an image. Anxiety can make sitting still difficult. If this is the case, suggest that the client listen to a relaxation tape while walking or rocking. In one instance, the only way one of my patients was able to focus on a tape was while marching around her hospital room.

One positive outcome of imagery, besides relaxation, is an increased sense of control, an impression that one has some recourse against the march of otherwise overwhelming and adverse events. "The Journey of Light" may be helpful in increasing the client's sense of control. The first part of the script involves relaxation and a suggestion to boost the immune system. The second part incorporates images of movement and is designed to impart a sense of mastery. The third part, the self-awareness section, is based on the writings of Stephen Levine (1991). Note, in this and other scripts, some elements of hypnotic induction. The author of "The Journey of Light" includes in the opening sentences of the script clear reference to her "signal" to enter a special state. Or, to put it another way, to anchor a quick technique for induction.

The guide can adapt "The Journey of Light" to be used in conjunction with chemotherapy by suggesting that the light represents the healing intentions of the physician who formulated the chemotherapy, the pharmacist who mixed it, and the nurse who administers it. As the line opens and the chemo either drips or is pushed into the patient's bloodstream, the guide can suggest a route by which the light from the chemo bag takes a healing journey throughout the body.

"The Journey of Light" and another guided imagery, "The Mountain Meditation," have been recorded, with harp accompaniment, by Patrice Rancour and Pegi Engelman-Loose. The two imageries, in tape or CD format, are available for purchase from the Arthur G. James Cancer Hospital and Richard J. Solove Research Institute by calling 614-293-6824 and asking for *Guided Meditations From The James.*

The Journey of Light

Patrice Rancour, MS, RN, CS

[Part 1: the induction portion of the imagery]

Find a comfortable position and close your eyes. Take a nice, deep breath. This is the signal breath. It signals to the body that you are moving into a special time and place set aside just for you. All subsequent breaths will be breathed normally in whatever way is most comfortable for you.

As you continue to breathe, feel the rise and fall of your chest as the air moves in, as the air moves out. As the air moves in, as the air moves out. As the air moves in, as the air moves out.

As you continue to breathe, you hear all sorts of sounds. Sounds from inside the room, sounds from outside the room. Nothing to change, nothing to judge. Whenever you feel the least bit distracted, just return your attention to your breathing.

As you continue to breathe, you will be having all sorts of thoughts. Thoughts about what has happened. Thoughts about what will happen. Nothing to change, nothing to judge. Just detach yourself from your thoughts and watch them as if they were a movie on a movie screen. Watch as the thoughts come and go, seemingly having a life of their own. Because right now, all you have to do is breathe.

And as you continue to breathe, let your body become an empty vessel and let your breath breathe you.

[Part 2: images of movement and suggestions to evoke a sense of mastery]

With your next breath, imagine that you inhale a luminous, healing light into the body. Bring it into your head and let it circulate into all the deep areas of the head, as well as the superficial scalp muscles. Especially, feel the light as it penetrates deeply into the muscles that surround the eyes, the mouth, and those very powerful jaw muscles. With each breath, feel these muscles soften, soften and relax. The light moving into places where pock-

60

ets of fear and doubt are held. Watch as the light dissolves these pockets of tension quickly, effortlessly, leaving behind a residue of heightened immune integrity, a "Live!" message.

With your next breath, allow the light to enter into the body and flow into the neck. Watch as the muscles in the neck begin to soften, soften and relax. As they do so, feel the throat open as the light dissolves pockets of fear and tension held there. And as the light circulates into the neck and throat, feel the residue of wholeness, peacefulness, and confidence it leaves behind.

Continuing to breathe, you inhale more of the healing light. You watch as it begins to flow into your shoulders, shoulders that have been asked to bear much. And, as the light floods into the shoulders, feel it penetrating deeply into these muscles and watch as they soften, soften and relax. And just when you think they couldn't possibly soften any further, watch as they let go even more.

Continuing to inhale more light into the body, you watch it begin to flow down your shoulders into your arms, your elbows, your wrists. It goes into your hands and out the very tips of your fingers, taking with it anything that does not belong, whether it be fear, anger, or doubt. It leaves behind only what is you.

With your next inhalation, take in more of the light and watch as it flows down the back of your neck and cascades down your back like a luminous waterfall. The light penetrates deeply into all the large and all the small muscles of the back. With each breath, you feel these muscles soften, soften and relax. And just when you think they couldn't possibly soften any further, you feel them let go. Left behind is a sense of peacefulness, a confidence that you are being upheld in the midst of all this.

Continuing to breathe, you take in more of the radiant light. You watch as it begins to pour into your chest from your throat, filling up all the little air sacs in your lungs, so that with each breath they become more vibrant, more radiant. As you breathe, you shift your attention to your heart space. This is the space in the chest where all the compassion you hold for others lies. As you breathe into and out of that space, you watch as it becomes more spacious, more expansive. So that finally and eventually, there is so much room in your heart that you can put yourself fully into your own heart, and you do so right now.

Continuing to breathe, you inhale more of the light and watch as it pours into the belly. With each breath, you silently repeat to yourself: soft belly, soft belly, soft belly. The light now bathes all the organs of digestion. It dissolves, quickly and effortlessly, pockets of fear and tension, leaving behind a residue of heightened immune integrity—a "Live!" message.

Continuing to inhale even more of the healing light, the light now begins to pour into your hips, your pelvis, and your buttocks. Watch as the light moves into any pockets of tension and fear and competently releases them. The light bathes all the organs of reproduction and elimination in the radiance of its glow.

Continuing to breathe, you watch as the light begins now to flow down your thighs, into your knees, into your calves and ankles. The light flows into those poor unsung heroes, the feet, until the feet are massaged in the radiance of the light. Now the whole body feels massaged in its glow. Watch as the light now shoots out the tips of the toes, taking with it anything that does not belong, whether it be fear, tension, or doubt. Anything that is not you. What is left behind is a residue of peacefulness, of wholeness—a "Live!" message.

And, as you continue to breathe, with each breath you feel the light in the body becoming stronger, more edified, more expansive. So that, as you continue breathing, the light radiates past the confines of the skin and fills up the room in which you are sitting. And as it continues to do so, it becomes difficult to discern where you end and everything else begins.

[Part 3: questions designed to heighten self-awareness]

And as you continue to breathe, silently ask yourself the following questions:
- Who is this who has a body, yet is not the body?
- Who is this who has feelings, yet is not the feelings?
- Who is this who has thoughts, yet is not the thoughts?

- Who is this constant space through which all these ever-changing bodily sensations, feelings, and thoughts flow like so many bubbles in a stream?
- Who is this watcher, the one who observes all?

Become aware of yourself as pure, conscious awareness. Be aware that you have the power to come from this place any time you wish and that you take this power with you everywhere you go. And the only thing you need to do to initiate this power is to take the initial signal breath.

Brookside

Warren P. Edwards, PhD

"Brookside" weaves real and metaphorical images to encourage the client to look inward for answers.

Begin by getting comfortable in the chair or bed. Just relax as well as you can. It works better if parts of your body are not resting on other parts: Place both feet side by side; let your hands rest softly. And close your eyes.

Now pay attention to your breathing. Let it begin to slow down

[Pace the client.]

. . . and become nice and even.

[Pause.]

Now take in a breath and hold it. Notice the tension in your chest, in your arms, starting to build. Now, let it go! Relax. Note how that tension is flowing out, just draining out now, from your arms. Your chest is more relaxed as your breathing returns to normal, slow, easy breathing. Pay attention to the nicer sensations of relaxation: perhaps some warmth; maybe some warm, wavy sensations; or tingling as your muscles get softer and more relaxed. As you breathe out, just think of the word *relax*.

[Pace the client.]

Relax. Let your thoughts go. Don't fight any thoughts that come in. Just let them pass on through, pass out of your mind again. As you go on relaxing, you feel calm and serene.

Now, imagine that you are resting beside a beautiful, peaceful brook, in a beautiful, magical place. Picture the details as clearly and fully as you can. Perhaps a majestic tree beside the brook, for you to rest under. See the leaves, the grass by the brook, the grassy field around you.

Notice the sounds: the sound of the brook; the breeze in the grass, in the trees.

Notice the position and the warmth of the sun, the cool earth beneath you. You can smell the earth, the grass, the trees and flowers growing near.

Hear birds calling overhead, the gentle rustling of the grass.

As you watch the birds, they are so free and graceful. Soaring. Veering. Listen to their distant cries. You begin to sway with them as you watch them. Soaring, gliding.

You look down and see that you, too, are flying. You are above the earth, sliding on the air currents, swooping, gliding. You see the earth below you, as you rise higher on a warm air current, soaring above the earth and trees and grass below.

Now you see that you're starting to lose altitude, starting to fall. But just focus your attention on the earth, push with your stare at the earth—will it away—and you soar upward as you realize you can push the earth away below you.

Now start to fly away from this scene. You're going to fly away to the west. Fly west, over the countryside. You see farm fields passing below you—dots of houses, rivers, and roads—quite distant below, and an occasional city.

[Pause.]

Now you are coming to some mountains. You see them rising ahead, and you fly high over them. The air is cooler here, flying higher than the mountains. See the mountain terrain far below.

And now you turn south. Soon you're flying over high plains, rivers, now deserts. Arid and vast as you glide onward.

[Pause.]

There below you, in the shimmering desert below, there are some shapes. Some rocks. A structure. A desolate, mysterious ruin in the desert. You swoop and circle downward, lower and closer to the ruin. You set down on a peculiar stone, an interesting stone. And there are other interesting stones and columns and parts of structures all around you. As you touch down on this stone, you become aware of an insight, something you realize about yourself and your life. Something that makes sense.

There may be other answers here. New wisdoms or age-old understandings. About nature, about love, and about life and you. You want to stay and explore here. As you touch another stone, your mind feels clear and open. You realize you could stay here a while and search for something that you need. You could find something to answer a question you have wanted to understand more fully. You may want to stay for several hours.

Explore—in the stones, in the sand, in the rubble of artifacts of lives lived as hard or as well as yours. In reality, you will spend only a few minutes here. You won't be gone long, but you will feel as though you have spent several hours in this magical, mysterious desert ruin. Go silently. Look and learn and wonder.

[Give the patient about 5 minutes of silence.]

Now slowly realize that you are dreaming by the side of the brook, in the beautiful field, in the midst of the grass and the breeze, with the birds overhead, swooping and soaring. You feel the warmth, the soft air, the cool earth. As you slowly awaken from your dream of flying, you wonder if you will remember what you learned when you return to this room. But you know you can return to the ruin—for rest, for renewal, or just to relax—again and again. So you feel fresh and ready to go back and on with your day.

[Pause briefly.]

Now I will count backward from five to one. When I get to three, open your eyes. When I reach two, begin to wiggle your toes and fingers. Ready?
Five, four, three: Open your eyes.
Two: Wiggle your toes and fingers. Look around.
One: You are now completely back in this room.

Scripts to Displace Pain

The symptom of pain often is combined with other symptoms. In many of the scripts that follow, which were designed to displace pain, the imagery involves the concept of a safe place. Evoking an image of a safe place or mental retreat is a common technique in pain-relieving imagery.

A Relaxing Place and Positive Imagery

Susan Ezra, RN, HNC

The script that follows is copyright 2001 by Beyond Ordinary Nursing and is used here with permission.

Begin by placing your body in a comfortable position, arms and legs uncrossed, back well supported. Now take three breaths, allowing each breath to relax you even more. Let the exhalation be a letting-go kind of breath, letting go of tension. With each "in" breath, take in what you need, and with each "out" breath, release anything you don't need.
Bring your attention to the top of your head. Feel your scalp relax, and let your brow soften and smooth out. Allow all the little muscles around your eyes to relax, and let any tension flow out through your cheeks as you exhale. Let your jaw relax. Imagine a wave of relaxation flowing down your shoulders—into your arms, elbows, forearms—all the way into your hands and fingers.
Now focus on your chest, releasing any tension around your heart or lungs. Relax the muscles around your ribs. Wrap that

relaxation around your back, and let a wave of relaxation travel all down the spine. Allow the muscles along the spine to lengthen and release. Soften and relax the buttocks and pelvis. Let the belly be very soft so that the breath moves easily down into the abdomen. Invite the legs to join in the relaxation now, as relaxation moves through the thighs, knees, calves, ankles, and feet. Let any last bit of tension or tightness just drain out through your feet and toes.

When you feel relaxed and comfortable, let me know with a nod of your head.

As your body remains relaxed and comfortable, imagine yourself in a very special place, someplace that is full of natural beauty, safety, and peace—maybe a place you have been to before, or maybe a place you want to create in your imagination. Take some time and let yourself be drawn to one place that is just right for you today. Give yourself some time to really be present there.

[In the paragraph that follows, the guide waits for responses to questions. This is the dialog aspect of the integrative process.]

What is it like there? What do you see? Are there any smells? Are there any sounds? What is the temperature? Where are you in this special place? How do you feel there? Take some time to enjoy being there.

While you are there, identify a specific quality or feeling that would be helpful in your life right now. It may be calmness, patience, peacefulness—choose one feeling that you are experiencing right now, here in your special place, that you wish to bring into your daily life. When you have chosen that quality, give yourself permission to experience it directly. Connect with the feeling, the emotion, and really experience it in your mind and body. Become aware of where you feel this quality most strongly in your body—perhaps in your chest or heart or belly, maybe in your head or hands. Wherever *you* feel that feeling most in your body, begin to let that feeling flow throughout your entire body, from the top of your head to the tips of your toes. Breathe in that quality with each "in" breath, and breathe it out to others in each exhalation. If you wish, let that feeling spill out into the space around you.

And now set that feeling or quality at a comfortable level for you right now. Know that you can access this quality whenever, wherever you wish. It is now registered in your mind and body.

Bring to mind a memory cue that will reconnect you with this feeling when you need it. Make this cue easy to remember. A cue could be a deep breath; a simple gesture, like placing your hand on the part of your body where you most strongly feel that quality; or a word or phrase that summons the feeling for you. When you have your cue, imagine a link between your cue and your desired quality, so that each time you use your cue, you will automatically experience this positive feeling.

In a few moments it will be time to come back into a waking state. Know that you can return to this place any time you want and take the quality with you when you leave it. Remember, you can call forth and use your quality at any time in your daily life. Now become aware of the current time and place. Begin to move your body. Take a deep breath, become aware of your external environment. Open your eyes, and feel refreshed and awake.

Creating a Space for Healing

Redwing Keyssar, RN, BA, OCN®

Please close your eyes. Imagine yourself going to a place that is *your* safe and sacred space. Only yours. It can be an indoor or outdoor space. It can be a real place that you have spent time in, or it can be a totally imagined safe space. It can have walls that protect you, or trees. It can be a cave, a river, a canyon, a church ... or simply your own living room. Take a few moments to get there. Notice the path that you take on your way.

When you have arrived in this space, slowly look all around it. Notice the shapes of the perimeter or walls. Notice the colors that surround you, and the textures. What is the temperature? Are there pictures on the walls? Are there plants around? Take a close look at the details of this place that is your sanctuary at the moment. As you look around, find a place to sit or lie down. A place to be comfortable. Take a few breaths there, breathing all the way into your belly, and breathing all the way out into the universe. Notice how you feel in this place. This is your place of safety. No one can access you here. No one and nothing can harm you.

Once you have gotten comfortable, imagine—in your mind's eye—your tumor.

[Other options: cancer, disease.]

Bring it into focus. It is simply an object you are looking at.

What color is it? What texture is it? Does it have a taste or smell? What size is it? Does it move, or is it stationary? Is it heavy or light? Take some time to just *be* in the same space with this entity. When you feel quite familiar with this object, simply put it aside, on the ground or on a table. Anywhere is fine.

And, in looking around your sanctuary again, in some particular place—on a wall or a tree, or hanging from on high—you notice there is a mirror. You walk over to the mirror and look closely into your own eyes. What do you see there? What is their color and shape? What is the expression in those eyes? Allow yourself to acknowledge this being that you are facing. Allow yourself to see the strength in this being's eyes. Allow yourself to really feel the power of this being—the strengths and weaknesses, the heart and soul. Tell that person in the mirror that you see a loving and healing being. Tell that person you see that person's strengths and understandings. Allow yourself to feel the healing powers in the eyes that are looking at you. And then ask this being for help.

Now, turning around to the object that is your cancer *[or tumor, or disease]*, surround that object with healing energy. Surround it with a color or texture or form or song that can encompass it, hold it, and allow it to experience healing.

Perhaps you need the object to disappear or change shape. Perhaps it becomes smaller. Perhaps it is just infused with this new and gentle energy that comes from your source.

Be with this healing for a moment. When you are ready, turn around. Before you begin your steps back on the path, take a moment to give thanks to this safe space. To this healing energy. Give thanks to yourself for spending time here today. Acknowledge the safety you feel, and know that you can come back here at any time.

Now, slowly begin your journey back. And when you are ready to come back to the everyday plane, take a few slow, deep breaths—all the way into your belly and all the way out—until you are ready to open your eyes.

When you have opened your eyes, please take the paper and crayons [*or pencils*] in front of you and draw a picture of your tumor and of the healing that you surrounded it with.

Reflecting on the Past

Monika Williamson, RN, BSN

The following script utilizes the concept of remembered wellness.

I'd like to start this relaxation session by having you close your eyes and take slow, deep breaths. Today I'm going to direct you to take a look into your past, back to an enjoyable time that is easy to access in your memory but which you may not have visited often.

These happy memories can have a healthy effect on your physical and emotional well-being. You can think of them as boosters for your relaxation.

To begin, step back to a time, not too long ago, at a family gathering or with friends. Perhaps this was a time of accomplishment or just a time of being together. There was occasional laughter or the sharing of information.

Now pick a favorite person. Look into his or her face, often smiling. Then look into that person's eyes . . . and freeze-frame this moment.

Look now to another member of the party, also searching that person's face. Put it in slow motion, either focusing on facial structures or how you are ever so comfortable with that person. Next, focus on that person's words. Perhaps the person is making a toast or voicing appreciation toward you or another loved one. Cherish these images for a few moments longer.

Now exit this scene and enter your memory bank again. Find another happy time. It may be a holiday or a time of new beginning. You see yourself as vibrant, experiencing the excitement, the warmth of people coming together that genuinely love and appreciate each other. Imagine yourself, voicing or showing appreciation to these individuals. Vow to shower them with kind words when they again enter your life. Relish some of these thoughts for a few minutes longer.

Last, take yourself back to your childhood, to a time of play and innocence. Look back at a time of magical beliefs, perhaps of St. Nick or fairies. Your young thoughts influenced your play as you pretended to be like your heroes. You may have held these beliefs for years, but often the most vivid memory was when something occurred that revealed these beliefs as fallacies. Still, you can now look back and remember how you enjoyed these young thoughts, and you no longer feel the sense of being crushed by the loss of them.

Time changes and reveals fallacies or changes in others, changes in yourself that you can overcome. Retain the good experiences with thoughts of reality and forgiveness. We all can overcome once-difficult times.

Hope Kindled

Katherine Brown-Saltzman, RN, MA

A script may be developed for an individual's specific needs or to emphasize a specific concept. The next script, as the title implies, was created to encourage hope.

Taking a deep breath, you stand at night's edge surrounded by darkness, tilting your head up to the sky above you. There, in the dark, are endless stars. Light carried across the universe. You steady yourself, feeling your feet firmly planted on the ground, as you take in the endless number, letting your eyes settle on the great distance. You fill yourself up with those small twinkling lights.

There, too, is the sliver of a moon, a fraction of its real size, you remind yourself. The moon is full, as full as it ever has been, just now beyond your reach. You become aware that all of this darkness is a mere shadow. You realize that, on the other side of the world, the sun's brightness fills the other half. Never is there total darkness, only the narrowed perception of light.

Now you lie down on the field of grass, letting the ground hold you, the sky above so immense that you open yourself to the awe and beauty. You allow yourself to expand into the space; you allow your breath to rise up in greeting. And then you watch as one star falls across the sky, gently tumbling through time and dipping down into your chest, where your heart opens to it. A gift filled with wishes and light, hope kindled and restored.

Little by little you become present to the room, with a slow, deep breath and an awareness of the gift now within you. Forever settled within you.

Imagery for Guidance

Janith S. Griffith, RN, BSN, OCN®

Get into a comfortable position. If you are sitting in a chair, feel the chair supporting you. Place both feet on the floor. Relax your hands on your lap. Close your eyes if having your eyes closed is comfortable for you.

Take three deep breaths, exhaling slowly after each one. Continue to relax each part of your body, starting with your feet and working to the top of your head. With each breath, feel that you are sinking into a deeper and more peaceful state. Become quiet throughout your entire body.

Now imagine that you are walking through a meadow filled with wildflowers. The grass is soft beneath your feet. As you walk along, the air fills with the faint sweetness of the flowers. The wind touches your face gently. You hear birds calling and feel the warmth of the sun upon your back.

The meadow leads you to an opening in the woods. A winding pathway leads down through the trees. You walk along the path, lulled by the sweet smells and the sounds of the woods. As the trees part, you see a sparkling lake ahead. There, beside the lake, is a comfortable rock to rest upon. You sit back, cradled by the rock, filled with contentment and peace.

As you sit there so peacefully, your wise one appears. Your own special wise one may take any form—man, woman, bird, insect, or other animal. This wise one has come to answer your questions and to provide guidance. Ask your wise one about anything that is troubling you. Be open and receptive to whatever your wise one has to offer you.

[Allow several minutes of quiet time.]

After your wise one has gone, sit quietly a few minutes before starting your journey back through the woods.

Once again, a birdsong floats along with you and the wind caresses your face. As you emerge from the woods into the meadow, the sun is warm upon your face and the sweetness of the flowers drifts on the breeze.

Gently now, let the meadow of wildflowers fade away. Again become aware of your body's presence here in this room. Feel the chair supporting you. Feel your feet planted firmly upon the floor. Know that, whenever you need guidance in the future, you can go on this journey within and find your own wise one again. Your wise one will guide you along life's pathway.

Take a deep breath, gently stretching. When you feel ready, open your eyes and return to this room.

Guided Imagery: Freedom

Janith S. Griffith, RN, BSN, OCN®

Take three deep, cleansing breaths. With each exhalation, let go of worries and cares. Continue to focus on your breath as you breathe slowly in and out. Allow yourself to become very comfortable in your body. As you breathe deeply, imagine that you are on a walk through a woodland.

You are on an open path that winds down through the woods. It is cool here. Your feet are cushioned by cedar chips along the trail. It is so peaceful. Overhead, the birds call quietly and sing to one another among the treetops.

As you walk along, you come to an open glade illuminated by a bright beam of sunshine. You sit down on a log to rest and look around at everything here in the open area. There, on a small bush, you see a cocoon. You gaze deeply at the cocoon.

Your thoughts turn to the caterpillar within that cocoon. How full of nourishment and knowledge he is—he will be able to grow and change into a completely new form. Now he rests there, warm and secure.

You are led to think of all that has nourished your own spirit up to this point and allowed for positive growth and change. Good food. Love and care from family and friends. Proper health care. Knowledge. Warmth. Shelter. All these thoughts surround you within your safe haven.

As you watch, the cocoon begins to open. A butterfly slowly emerges, stretching his wings and beginning his life's journey, free of all that held him enclosed in the past.

As the butterfly flutters off through the woods, you are drawn along the pathway behind it. You walk along, always keeping the fluttering colors just in sight.

You see that now the path through the secure wood is leading you back into the everyday world.

You take three deep breaths as you return: With each breath that you breathe in, reach deep inside yourself, for you know the knowledge you need to be able to break free of your own inner struggles or pain. The knowledge is there with you. You breathe out worry and care, leaving them behind.

As you leave the sheltering woods, you *do* find the courage to break free.

You breathe deeply . . . and emerge into the light.

Heavenly Scene

Hazel A. Jackson, RN, MN

The author of this script acknowledges the contributions of Sister Alice Butler and Reverend E. Jackson. The script was inspired by Debra Repa.

You see a bright light. You look in the direction of the light. It is a star. You follow the star. Suddenly you are standing before a river of crystal-clear water.

You undress and walk into the crystal-clear water. It offers no resistance; there is no sensation of fear. The water feels cool and wet. Go deeper and deeper. You are now in the water up to your neck. Sniff the water; it has no smell. Taste the water; it has no taste. Take a deep breath. Submerge. There is no fear, no pressure, no ringing in your ears. You feel baptized by the water. Stand in the river, feel the sand along the bottom. Take a deep breath. The clear, pure air enters your lungs easily, without resistance. The air is light and nourishing. It gives you a feeling of newness, of peace. You feel like a new person as you leave the river of crystal-clear water. Your skin dries from the warmth of the breeze.

An angel is standing on the shore with hands extended, holding a garment of white silk. The angel drapes you in the silk cloth. You look radiant. You feel like a little girl or boy. You place your hand in the angel's hand.

You walk through 12 gates surrounding a great city. The walls are jasper, garnished with precious stones. The city is pure gold. Your eyes become teary, you feel a hand gently wiping the tears away. There are no tears, no pain, headaches, fear, or suffering in this beautiful city. You feel loved and very special. You drink from the fountain of life. The water has no taste, no smell. You bite into a fig from the tree of life. It tastes and settles comfortably into your stomach. Pull a leaf from the healing tree. Crumble the leaf in the palm of your hand. Feel a warm sensation traveling up your arms, up your neck and head, down your body, and out through your toes. What is left? Healthy, functioning cells.

You feel loved. You are a child of God. You feel the presence of arms around you, and you know you are not alone. You will never be alone. You are confident that you can handle any challenge, overcome any obstacle. You absorb the beauty, peace, love, and tranquility. It's time to leave now. It's okay to leave because you can come to your special place any time you want by taking several slow, deep breaths, relaxing, and seeing the bright light.

I will count from five to one. You will open your eyes on the count of one, feeling loved, comfortable, confidant of your ability to handle life's challenges, and relaxed. Or, if it's sleep time, you will be able to go into a restful sleep.

I'm going to bring you back to the room now.

Five: You are coming back slowly.

Four: You feel relaxed and refreshed.

Three: You feel loved, special, and alive.

Two, one: Open your eyes.

Numbers

Warren P. Edwards, PhD

The script that follows may be particularly helpful for clients who enjoy word images.

As you begin to relax, I want you to remember back when you first went to school. You learned your numbers before you went to school. First, you learned the word that went with the number, what you said as you unfolded, one by one, the fingers of your fist: One, two, three, etc. As you unfolded each finger and said the word, you could picture the number, the written digit that went with each word, and you had different feelings about each digit.

The number one was perfect and friendly, its appearance resembled its meaning, and it was reassuring in that regard.

The number two looked more complicated than it was. But at least–if you drew it schematically, like a letter Z, and considered the middle line a way to get from the top to the bottom lines–it, like the number one, also resembled its meaning.

Three was pleasing. Its three points made it easy to understand, easy to remember. You could add two three's by counting up their six points.

Four, if you wrote it with an open top, had four points. The system broke down with the numeral five. But, since five was half of 10, quick and accurate things could be done with it. Shortcuts to more difficult problems were available by using the number five, so it was worth the trouble. Six, although it was an even number, resembled an odd number because it was curved like three and like five.

Seven was the most difficult design. It was hard to picture the number of units it represented. Sometimes the best you could do was six and one, or five units and two units next to none. Picturing four units and three units was most difficult.

The number eight was appealing because it was paradoxical: It had the curves of an odd number but, because it was vertically symmetrical, it was an appropriate symbol for an even number.

Nine. The only way to deal with nine was as one less than 10. And considering how high 10 was, you did pretty well with it. Two 10's were 20; therefore, two nine's were two less than 20, or 18. This worked all the way up to nine nine's. Nine nine's were nine less than nine 10's, or 81.

Zero, like one, was perfect.

One day, when you were four or five years old and thinking about numbers, you recognized that the series of zero to nine paralleled the series 10 to 19, 20 to 29, 30 to 39, etc. You felt a bit of power and understanding where it had not been before. Sometime later, on a sheet of paper, you wrote the numbers 1 to 100 and 101 to 200, 201 to 300. If anyone checked your list for accuracy, you were confident that the numbers and their sequence were correct because you understood the inherent logic and system in them.

The teachers may have announced that the numeral four would now be made with a closed top. That wouldn't matter, now that you understood the system. Your thinking about how the numbers should be drawn had changed, but the system had not. Your understanding of the system was the important thing, because you had discovered the decimal system for yourself. You knew the relationships expressed in it.

But, when you were asked to multiply, you ran through rote memorized tables. In time, you lost your feel for the numeric architecture, and mathematics became a less rich subject. You may have even forgotten parts of the multiplication tables—6 x 7, 7 x 8, 8 x 4—and you may have done poorly on tests.

However, if you sit down and work out your own table again, using the system that you still understand, and work out the answers—if you commit that process to memory again—your interest in numbers will return to that mystical level with which you first encountered them. In your 60s, you will wonder if the recurrence of numbers in the mid-80s is your history multiplied to the end of your life in an equally mystical, systematic way.

It can be good to remember these things and wonder at the magic of your mind. You may continue with this thought or bring your attention to your breathing, your place in this room, and bring your mind back to the present.

REFERENCE

Levine, S. (1991). *Guided meditations, explorations and healings.* New York: Anchor Books.

Chapter 4

Guided Imagery Resources

Guided Imagery Resources

Mary Jane Ott, MN, MA, RNCS

This chapter will provide listings of resources that may be useful to clinicians with an interest in guided imagery. The listings are categorized by resource type: articles and book chapters, books, journals, sources of audiotapes and other products, organizations that provide imagery education, professional nursing organizations that have imagery as a primary focus, and organizations that focus on hypnosis.

ARTICLES AND BOOK CHAPTERS

The articles cited in this section are representative of the literature or have made significant contributions to it. Some offer theoretical frameworks, others provide research results, and still others offer sample scripts or clinical exemplars. Though the emphasis is on oncology, the articles discuss a variety of specialties. The intent in offering the list is to provide a beginning point for the reader. From this point, he or she can choose sources depending on interest rather than having to review an exhaustive list of what is available.

Baider, L., Uziely, B., & De-Nour, A.K. (1994). Progressive muscle relaxation and guided imagery in cancer patients. *General Hospital Psychiatry, 16,* 340–347.

Broome, M.E., Rehwaldt, M., & Fogg, L. (1998). Relationships between cognitive behavioral techniques, temperament, observed distress, and pain reports in children and adolescents during lumbar puncture. *Journal of Pediatric Nursing, 13*(1), 48–54.

Daake, D.R., & Gueldner, S.H. (1989). Imagery instruction and the control of postsurgical pain. *Applied Nursing Research, 2*(3), 114–120.

Deisch, P., Soukup, S.M., Adams, P., & Wild, M.C. (2000). Guided imagery: Replication study using coronary artery bypass graft patients. *Nursing Clinics of North America, 35,* 417–425.

Dossey, B. (1995). Complementary modalities (Part 3): Using imagery to help your patients heal. *American Journal of Nursing, 95*(6), 40–47.

Eller, L.S. (1999). Guided imagery interventions for symptom management. *Annual Review of Nursing Research, 17,* 57–84.

Fawzy, N.W. (1995). A psychoeducational nursing intervention to enhance coping and affective state in newly diagnosed malignant melanoma patients. *Cancer Nursing, 18,* 427–438.

Foertsch, C.E., O'Hara, M.W., Stoddard, F.J., & Kealey, G.P. (1998). Treatment-resistant pain and distress during pediatric burn-dressing changes. *Journal of Burn Care and Rehabilitation, 19,* 219–224.

Frank, J.M. (1985). The effects of music therapy and guided visual imagery on chemotherapy-induced nausea and vomiting. *Oncology Nursing Forum, 12*(5), 47–52.

Giedt, J.F. (1997). Guided imagery. A psychoneuroimmunological intervention in holistic nursing practice. *Journal of Holistic Nursing, 15*(2), 112–127.

Hoffart, M.B., & Keene, E.P. (1998). The benefits of visualization. *American Journal of Nursing, 98*(12), 44–47.

Keller, V.E. (1995). Management of nausea and vomiting in children. *Journal of Pediatric Nursing, 10,* 280–286.

Kolcaba, K., & Fox, C. (1999). The effects of guided imagery on comfort of women with early stage breast cancer undergoing radiation therapy. *Oncology Nursing Forum, 26,* 67–72.

Kwekkeboom, K.L., Huseby-Moore, K., & Ward, S. (1998). Imaging ability and effective use of guided imagery. *Research in Nursing and Health, 21,* 189–198.

Kwekkeboom, K.L., Maddox, M.A., & West, T. (2000). Measuring imaging ability in children. *Journal of Pediatric Health Care, 14,* 297–303.

Lambert, S.A. (1996). The effects of hypnosis/guided imagery on the postoperative course of children. *Developmental and Behavioral Pediatrics, 17,* 307–310.

Lambert, S.A. (1999). Distraction, imagery, and hypnosis: Techniques for management of children's pain. *Journal of Child and Family Nursing, 2*(1), 5–15.

Lee, L.H., & Olness, K. (1996). Effects of self-induced mental imagery on autonomic reactivity in children. *Developmental and Behavioral Pediatrics, 17,* 323–327.

Lee, R. (1999). Guided imagery as supportive therapy in cancer treatment. *Alternative Medicine Alert: A Clinician's Guide to Alternative Therapies, 2*(6), 61–64.

Levitan, A.A. (1992). The use of hypnosis with cancer patients. *Psychiatric Medicine, 10*(1), 119–131.

Liossi, C., & Hatira, P. (1999). Clinical hypnosis versus cognitive behavioral training for pain management with pediatric cancer patients undergoing bone marrow aspirations. *The International Journal of Clinical and Experimental Hypnosis, 47*(2), 104–114.

Moore, R.J., & Spiegel, D. (1999). Uses of guided imagery for pain control by African-American and white women with metastatic breast cancer. *Integrative Medicine, 2*(2/3), 115–126.

Ott, M.J. (1996). Imagine the possibilities! Guided imagery with toddlers and pre-schoolers. *Pediatric Nursing, 22*(1), 34–38.

Ott, M.J. (1997). A day at the beach. *Gastroenterology Nursing, 20*(4), 141–142.

Pederson, C. (1995). Effect of imagery on children's pain and anxiety during cardiac catheterization. *Journal of Pediatric Nursing, 10,* 365–374.

Post-White, J. (1998). Imagery. In M. Snyder & R. Lindquist (Eds.), *Complementary/alternative therapies in nursing* (3rd ed.) (pp. 103–122). New York: Springer.

Post-White, J., & Johnson, M. (1991). Complementary nursing therapies in clinical oncology practice: Relaxation and imagery. *Dimensions in Oncology Nursing, 5*(2), 15–20.

Schaub, B.G., & Dossey, B.M. (2000). Imagery: Awakening the inner healer. In B.M. Dossey, L. Keegan, & C.E. Guzzetta (Eds.), *Holistic nursing: A handbook* (3rd ed.) (pp. 539–581). Gaithersburg, MD: Aspen.

Spiegel, D., & Moore, R. (1997). Imagery and hypnosis in the treatment of cancer patients. *Oncology, 11,* 1179–1190.

Steggles, S., Damore-Petingola, S., Maxwell, J., & Lightfoot, N. (1997). Hypnosis for children and adolescents with cancer: An annotated bibliography, 1985–1995. *Journal of Pediatric Oncology Nursing, 14*(1), 27–32.

Tusek, D., Church, J.M., & Fazio, V.W. (1997). Guided imagery as a coping strategy for perioperative patients. *Association of Operating Room Nurses Journal, 66,* 644–649.

Tusek, D., Church, J.M., Strong, S., Grass, J.A., & Fazio, V.W. (1997). Guided imagery: A significant advance in the care of patients undergoing elective colorectal surgery. *Diseases of the Colon and Rectum, 40*(2), 172–178.

Van Fleet, S. (2000). Relaxation and imagery for symptom management: Improving patient assessment and individualizing treatment. *Oncology Nursing Forum, 27,* 501–510.

Vines, S.W. (1988). The therapeutics of guided imagery. *Holistic Nursing Practice, 2*(3), 34–44.

Wallace, K.G. (1997). Analysis of recent literature concerning relaxation and imagery interventions for cancer pain. *Cancer Nursing, 20*(2), 79–87.

Wallace, S. (1999). Guided imagery: Using visualization to heal. *Alternative and Complementary Therapies, 5*(3), 175–176.

BOOKS

Achterberg, J. (1985). *Imagery in healing: Shamanism and modern medicine.* Boston: New Science Library/Shambhala.

Achterberg, J., Dossey, B., & Kolkmeier, L. (1994). *Rituals of healing: Using imagery* New York: Bantam Books.

Belknap, M. (1994). *Taming more dragons.* Boulder, CO: The Village Printer.

Battino, R. (2000). *Guided imagery and other approaches to healing.* Bancyfelin, Wales: Crown House Publishing.

Bush, C.A. (1995). *Healing imagery and music.* Portland, OR: Rudra Press.

Clark, C.C. (1999). *Integrating complementary procedures into practice.* New York: Springer.

Clark, C.C. (Ed.). (1999). *Encyclopedia of complementary health practice.* New York: Springer.

Curran, E. (2001). *Guided imagery.* Hillsboro, OR: Beyond Words Publishing.

Dossey, B.M., Keegan, L., & Guzzetta, C.E. (Eds.). (2000). *Holistic nursing: A handbook for practice* (3rd ed.). Gaithersburg, MD: Aspen.

Garth, M. (1991). *Starbright: Meditations for children.* New York: Harper-Collins.

Garth, M. (1992). *Moonbeam: A book of meditations for children.* North Blackburn, Victoria, Australia: CollinsDove.

Garth, M. (1994). *Sunshine: More meditations for children.* North Blackburn, Victoria, Australia: CollinsDove.

Gawain, S. (1995). *Creative visualization* (rev. ed.). Novato, CA: Nataraj Publishing.

Guzzetta, C.E. (1998). *Essential readings in holistic nursing.* Gaithersburg, MD: Aspen.

Hammond, D. (Ed.). (1990). *Handbook of hypnotic suggestions and metaphor.* New York: Norton.

Huddleston, P. (1996). *Prepare for surgery, heal faster: Guide of mind body techniques.* Cambridge, MA: Angel River Press.

Jonas, W.B., & Levin, J.S. (Eds.). (1999). *Essentials of complementary and alternative medicine.* Baltimore: Lippincott Williams & Wilkins.

Levine, S. (1991). *Guided meditations, explorations and healings.* New York: Doubleday.

Lusk, J.T. (Ed.). (1992). *Thirty scripts for relaxation, imagery and inner healing.* Duluth, MN: Whole Person Associates.

Miller, E. (1997). *Deep healing: The essence of mind/body medicine.* Carlsbad, CA: Hay House.

Murdock, M. (1987). *Spinning inward: Using guided imagery with children for learning, creativity and relaxation.* Boston: Shambhala.

Naparstek, B. (1994). *Staying well with guided imagery.* New York: Warner.

Olness, K., & Kohen, D. (1996). *Hypnosis and hypnotherapy with children* (3rd ed.) New York: Guilford Press.

Rossman, M. (2000). *Guided imagery for self-healing.* Novato, CA: H.J. Kramer.

Simonton, C., Simonton, S., & Creighton, J. (1978). *Getting well again.* Los Angeles: Tarcher.

Thondup, T. (1996). *The healing power of the mind: Simple meditation exercises for health, well-being, and enlightenment.* Boston: Shambhala.

Thondup, T. (2000). *Boundless healing: Meditation exercises to enlighten the mind and heal the body.* Boston: Shambhala.

RELATED JOURNALS

The following journals do not have guided imagery as a significant focus. Their editors appreciate its importance, however, and the journals are resources that support and expand knowledge for clinicians by sometimes offering articles of importance related to guided imagery. Each journal title is followed by contact information regarding the organization that publishes it.

Alternative Therapies in Health and Medicine
InnoVision Communications, LLC
169 Saxony Road, Suite 104
Encinitas, CA 92024
Telephone: 866-828-2962
Web site: www.alternative-therapies.com

American Journal of Clinical Hypnosis
American Society of Clinical Hypnosis
130 E. Elm Court, Suite 201
Roselle, IL 60172
Telephone: 630-980-4740
Web site: www.asch.net/journal.htm

Holistic Nursing Practice
Aspen Publications
200 Orchard Ridge Drive
Gaithersburg, MD 20878
Telephone: 301-417-7500
Web site: www.nursingcenter.com/journals/index.cfm

International Journal of Clinical and Experimental Hypnosis
Society for Clinical and Experimental Hypnosis
P.O Box 642114
Pullman, WA 99164-2114
Telephone: 509-335-2097
Web site: http://sunsite.utk.edu/IJCEH/ijcehframes.htm

Journal of Holistic Nursing
Sage Publications
2455 Teller Road
Thousand Oaks, CA 91320
Telephone: 805-499-0721
Web site: www.sagepub.com

SOURCES OF AUDIOTAPES AND OTHER PRODUCTS RELATING TO GUIDED IMAGERY

Exceptional Cancer Patients
1302 Chapel St.
New Haven, CT 06511
Telephone: 203-865-8392
Contact: Bernie Siegel

Fanlight Productions
4196 Washington St., Suite #2
Boston, MA 92131
Telephone: 617-469-4999
Video: *Finding Your Way*

Health Associates, Inc.
P.O. Box 220
Big Sur, CA 93920
Fax: 408-667-0248
Contacts: Jeanne Achterberg, Frank Lawlis

Image Paths, Inc.
891 Moe Drive, Suite C
Akron, OH 44310
Toll-free telephone: 800-800-8661
E-mail: hjtapes@aol.com
Web site: www.healthjourneys.com
Contact: Belleruth Naparstek

The Imagery Store
Academy for Guided Imagery
P.O. Box 2070
Mill Valley, CA 94942
Telephone: 415-389-9324
Toll-free telephone: 800-726-2070
Fax: 415-389-9342
Web site: www.healthy.net/agi
Contacts: Martin Rossman, David Bresler

Mind/Body Medical Institute
Attention: Tapes
110 Francis St., Suite 1A
Boston, MA 02215
Telephone: 617-632-9525
Fax: 617-632-7383
Contact: Herbert Benson

MindWorks for Children
P.O. Box 2493
Cambridge, MA 02238-2493
Telephone: 617-876-5585
Web site: www.mindworksforchildren.com
Contact: Roxanne Daleo

Petrea King Collection
P.O. Box 190
Bundanoon, NSW 2578
Australia
Telephone: 61-2-4883-6599
Fax: 61-2-4883-6755
E-mail: pktapes@questforlife.com.au
Web site: www.questforlife.com.au/petreaking
Contact: Petrea King

Simonton Cancer Center
P.O. Box 890
Pacific Palisades, CA 90272
Telephone: 310-459-4434
Contact: O. Carl Simonton

Source Cassette Learning Systems, Inc.
131 E. Placer St.
P.O. Box 6028
Auburn, CA 95604
Toll-free telephone: 800-528-2737
Toll-free fax: 800-888-1840
Web site: www.DrMiller.com
Contact: Emmett Miller

Warm Rock Tapes
P.O. Box 108
Chamisal, NM 87521
Toll-free telephone: 800-731-HEAL (4325)
Contacts: Steve and Ondrea Levine

ORGANIZATIONS THAT PROVIDE EDUCATIONAL
PROGRAMS ABOUT GUIDED IMAGERY

Academy for Guided Imagery
P.O. Box 2070
Mill Valley, CA 94942
Toll-free telephone: 800-726-2070
Fax: 415-389-9342
Web site: www.healthy.net/agi
Contacts: Marty Rossman, David Bresler

The American Institute for Mental Imagery
351 E. 84th St., Suite 10D
New York, NY 10028
Telephones: 212-988-7750, 212-534-4373

Beyond Ordinary Nursing[a]
P.O. Box 8177
Foster City, CA 94404
Voice mail: 650-570-6157
Fax: 650-570-6157
E-mail: ncpii@aol.com
Web site: www.imageryrn.com
Contact: Susan Ezra
[a] Offers a nurses certificate program in imagery that is endorsed by
the American Holistic Nurses' Association

Center for Mind-Body Medicine
5225 Connecticut Ave. NW, Suite 414
Washington, DC 20001
Telephone: 212-966-7338
Web site: www.cmbm.org

Certification Program in Clinical Imagery and Clinical Meditation
New York Psychosynthesis Institute
2 Murray Court
Hunting, NY 117443
Telephone: 516-673-0293
Fax: 516-423-2684
E-mail: rschaub@ix.netcom.com

Guided Imagery, Inc.
2937 Lamplight Lane
Willoughby Hill, OH 44094
Telephone: 440-944-9292
Fax: 440-944-1830
E-mail: imageryg@stratos.net
Web site: www.guidedimageryinc.com
Contact: Diane L. Tusek

International Association of Interactive Imagery
300920 Lanes Turn Road
Eugene, OR 97401
Web site: www.iaii.org

PROFESSIONAL NURSING ORGANIZATIONS WITH GUIDED IMAGERY AS A SIGNIFICANT FOCUS

American Holistic Nurses' Association
P.O. Box 2130
Flagstaff, AZ 86003
Toll-free telephone: 800-278-AHNA (2462)
Fax: 520-526-2752
Web site: www.ahna.org

Nurse Healers–Professional Associates International
3760 S. Highland Drive, Suite 429
Salt Lake City, UT 84106
Telephone: 801-273-3399
Fax: 509-693-3537
E-mail: NH-PAI@Therapeutic-Touch.org
Web site: www.therapeutic-touch.org

ORGANIZATIONS THAT FOCUS ON HYPNOSIS

Hypnosis, unlike guided imagery, requires specialized training and supervised experience.

American Institute of Hypnotherapy
1805 E. Garry Ave., Suite 100
Santa Ana, CA 92705
Telephone: 714-261-6400

American Pacific University
615 Piikoi St., Suite 501
Honolulu, HI 96814
telephone: 808-596-7765
Web site: www.ampac.edu

American Society of Clinical Hypnosis
130 E. Elm Court, Suite 201
Roselle, IL 60172
telephone: 630-980-4740
Web site: www.asch.net

International Medical and Dental Hypnotherapy Association
4110 Edgeland Ave., Suite 800
Royal Oak, MI 48073
Telephone: 313-549-5594
Toll-free telephone: 800-257-5467 (outside Michigan only)
Web site: www.learnhypnosis.com/imdha.htm

The National Guild of Hypnotists
P.O. Box 308
Merrimack, NH 03054
Telephone: 603-429-9438
Web site: www.ngh.net

Society for Clinical and Experimental Hypnosis
P.O. Box 642114
Pullman, WA 99164-2114
Telephone: 509-335-2097
Web site: http://sunsite.utk.edu/IJCEH/ijcehframes.htm

Index

INDEX

The letter t *after a page number indicates a table; the letter* f *indicates a figure.*

A

Academy for Guided Imagery, 87, 89
active imagery, 6, 13
acute pain, imagery management of, 11
acute stress, immune response to, 5
adrenocorticotropic hormone, released during stress, 4
Alternative Therapies in Health and Medicine, 86
American Holistic Nurses' Association, 90
The American Institute for Mental Imagery, 89
American Institute of Hypnotherapy, 91
American Journal of Clinical Hypnosis, 86
American Medical Association (AMA), and hypnosis, recognition as therapeutic tool, 4
American Pacific University, 91
American Psychological Association (APA), and hypnosis, recognition as therapeutic tool, 4
American Society of Clinical Hypnosis, 91
anxiety
  during chemotherapy, 12
  in children, 9
  increased during imagery, 7
  scripts to displace, 59–66
ASIST (A Self-directed Inner Search Therapy), 31–35, 39
assessment, prior to guided imagery, 8
audiotapes, of imagery scripts, 59, 87–89

auditory images, creation of, 47–48
Awakening Intuition, 30

B

Beyond Ordinary Nursing, 66, 89
bone marrow biopsy, pain management for, 10–11
breathing techniques, 6, 54–56
  for children, 10
  difficulties during, 7–8
"Brookside" script, 63–66
Brown-Saltzman, Katherine, imagery script by, 71–72

C

cancer outcomes, imagery and, 13–14
cancer pain, imagery management of, 11–2
Center for Mind-Body Medicine, ix–x, 89
"centering" exercise, 5–6
  and breathing difficulties, 7–8
  script for, 50
Certification Program in Clinical Imagery and Clinical Meditation, 90
chemotherapy, symptom management during, 12
childbirth, imagery used during, 9
children
  and guided imagery
    anxiety relieved with, 9
    length of sessions, 5
    and pain management, 10
    relaxed vs. active, 6
  hypnotic ability of, 7
  relaxation breathing for, 10
chronic stress, immune response to, 5

W

Warm Rock Tapes, 89

Wellspring (support program), 25, 30

Williamson, Monika, imagery script by, 70–71

word images, 47, 76–78